"GOOD LORD!"
CRIED THE WOODCHUCK

"GOOD LORD!"
CRIED THE WOODCHUCK

Then what happened?

P.G. Wheatley

Gourd Head & Grant Publishing

DEDICATION

THIS IS THE DEDICATION, NOT THE START OF THE BOOK.

I, Peter G. Wheatley, being of sound mind do hereby dedicate this book to the following:

To Grace who has been and **is** my everything.

To son Tommy, for all the help to daddy and mommy.

To Mark Twain who said, "The older I get, the more clearly I remember things that never happened."

To Nina's husband, Big **Good** John Searcy, whose encouragement after reading "MARRY MERRY MARY CHRISTMAS?" gave me the desire to share some more of my life. (My apologies to the late Jimmie Dean the sausage king who wrote and performed Big **Bad** John.)

To all of the Dallas Cheerleaders for giving me a reason to watch the Cowboys.

To talking woodchucks for spicing up my title.

Table of Contents

BOOK ONE   **17**

Colorado   **17**

Easter Break   17

Drive to School   20

Back on Campus   23

The Decision   27

Petrarch Grant Wheatley III   30

Wedding Day   32

Honeymoon Motel   39

E. T. Phone Home   42

The Flight   48

Denver Summer   51

On Top of Spaghetti   58

Hilpert's Pants   61

BOOK TWO   **69**

California   **69**

California or Bust   69

Yucca Valley   73

Angel One   78

House on the Hill   81

Yucca Valley Elementary   84

Mr. Fitness   86

Reeves   88

Professional Organizations   89

House Hunting 90

Back At the Ranch (Gallup) 91

Neckties 95

Yucca Valley Snow 97

"The Desert Wind" 99

Glasses 112

Baseball 116

Disneyland 121

The Big Bear Went Over the Mountain 123

Baby Runs 126

Baby Birth Day 127

After Birth 139

Little Fish 141

Tommy Terrific 143

First Christmas 143

Maria 146

By The Time I Get To Phoenix 149

Petrarch and Laura 150

Ringy Dingy Dingy 154

Baby D. J. 156

Time to Go 166

The Rescue 173

Bye Bye Boxer 178

BOOK THREE **195**

Colorado Again **195**

Wild Bill 195

Chatty Kathy 198

Life In Fort Collins 205

Best of Times/ Worst of Times 207

Abandoned Ski Resort 209

Lucky 215

Officer Wheatley 216

Square Dance 217

Badgers 222

Dilemma 226

Migration 227

ABOUT THE AUTHOR **235**

GREETING

THIS IS THE GREETING, NOT THE START OF THE BOOK.

HELLO EVERYBODY.

Here we go again: another book. My first book "Marry Merry Mary Christmas?" covered a period of three weeks and was 183 pages. This book covers 520 weeks and is only 218 pages (Go figure).

But you will find it interesting if, like the late Walter Woodchuck, you'd like to know what happened next in Wheatley's Weird, Wacky, and Wonderful World.

WARD

THIS IS THE WARD. NOT THE START OF THE BOOK. I have divided the ward into forward, middle-ward, and backward. Perhaps the one in the center should be called the "mental" ward.

My first book ended with Grace and Pete finally getting together on New Year's Day in 1965. If you haven't read it yet, I would recommend reading it first. And . . . I just happen to know of someone who has several thousand copies of "Marry Merry Mary Christmas?" by P.G. Wheatley. He's either a fan, or P.G. Wheatley himself.

(You know, P.G. really doesn't sound like me. **Maybe** I'll call myself just plain Pete Wheatley from now on because that is how I think of myself. And that is how I was known for my first twenty-three years.)

When it was time for school to start again after that magical holiday of Christmas 1964, Grace's Uncle Bob and Aunt Betty drove us the 200 miles to Durango. (In the first book I called them Uncle Fezziwig and wife. I also called them Bert and Belle. I had not **really** got to know this wonderful couple yet. (I did a lot of name changing in the books to protect people's privacy. --PG)

MIDDLE-WARD

I bet you are wondering where I got the title for this book. The book's purpose is to fill in the ten years from the magic Christmas of 1964 to our move to Cousins Valley, a land where 95% of the people were Navajo, and we had to travel 8 miles to reach the nearest paved road, then twenty miles to reach the nearest town.

"The Next Ten Years" seemed a boring title as did **"Then What Happened?"** I wanted something to catch your eye. Then I remembered what Principal Milligan told me the woodchuck said when the owl grabbed him. It was an attention grabbing, **"GOOD LORD!"**

I worked as a school teacher in four different school districts under five different principals. They were all good, but different. The one with the most charisma was Principal Milligan. He came during my last year in Yucca Valley, when Principal Marvin moved up to the mid-school.

Whenever anything unusual happened, whether it was good or whether it was bad, Principal Milligan would say in a voice usually restricted to a golfer getting a hole-in-one, (good) or blowing a 12 inch putt, (bad) "GOOD LORD, CRIED THE WOODCHUCK!" It wasn't too long before all the teachers, janitors, students, bus drivers, and some parents were saying, "GOOD LORD, CRIED THE WOODCHUCK!"

I've heard that imitation is the sincerest form of flattery. It must be true. We all loved this man Milligan and wanted to please him and be like him. Judging by the title of this book, I guess I still do.

BACKWARDS

The book starts back at the end of the Christmas break with Pete and Grace at her parents' home 30 miles southwest of Gallup, New Mexico.

It had snowed again and more was predicted. The greatest generation (parents & pirates) did not want Gracie on the road in my tiny little Nash Metropolitan. Besides that, the Metro was too small to carry all her luggage. The only thing Grace hadn't packed was a shovel. This oversight could have been catastrophic if we were attacked by a foreign power and needed to quickly dig a foxhole. I imagine, Grace felt guilty because of this oversight, as she usually likes to be prepared for any emergencies.

Riding anywhere with Aunt Betty was like riding with an excellent tour guide. Every mile reminded her of some historical or personal fact that made the trip so much more interesting and fun. If I hadn't been an impoverished, in debt college student, I would have offered her a large tip at the completion of the trip.

Bob's contributions to the conversation and discussion were grunts, snorts, and observations like: "Looks like it's going to snow." "I don't see why Malin (Sarge) couldn't have driven them." "There's a snowflake." "There's another." "Oh Dear."

When we arrived on campus, I witnessed the fastest unloading of a car possible. Like I said, more snow had been predicted and Bob had actually seen and documented a snowflake or two and was anxious to get back home. I took fifteen seconds to thank Aunt Betty for her narrative during the ride and stepped out of the vehicle. There to greet me were my skis, boots, poles, backpack, and Grace's five suitcases. These objects were waiting for me on the curb. Like I said, Uncle Bob was anxious to get home. The sky was darkening, and the wind picking up. We could tell the predicted snow was about to become a reality.

Bob and I carried two suitcases a piece and Grace one over to the girl's dorm at a trot, while Aunt Betty stayed by the truck guarding my stuff. (In my 60 years being married to Grace, we have traveled to many many places all over the world, and that is the least amount of luggage she has ever taken.)

When Bob and I got back to the truck, they kindly helped me get my backpack on, loaded all the rest of my stuff in my arms, and gave me a shove in the right direction. I felt like I was Jeeves again or a pack mule.[1] When I got to the dorm door, I turned back to shout that I had made it, but they were gone, most likely all the way off the mesa.

Well, I'll thank them for the ride and the hernia when I go down at Spring Break to pick up my car, I thought. (They actually beat the storm home.)

CONGRATULATIONS! **YOU** MADE IT. THE REAL BOOK BEGINS NOW, ON THE NEXT PAGE.

---

[1] "Marry Merry Mary Christmas" Page 164

Fort Lewis Chapel

BOOK ONE

Colorado

We both could have died seven pages from now. I ended up with a broken foot and Grace (in her own words) . . . "slightly embarrassed." Let me tell you about "slightly embarrassed."

Easter Break

Grace and I took the bus to Gallup from Durango and were picked up by Mrs. Cousins and Auntie and driven out to the ranch.

I was relieved to see that there was not even a speck of snow and nothing major had been done to my little car. All the tires still had some air in them, and I was able to get the writing in lipstick off after only an hour of scrubbing and two trips through the carwash in town. Someone had written comments all over the car with the expensive lipstick: the kind that advertises that it won't come off. The only prose I remember at this late date is, "I am not getting fat, you little pipsqueak."

Spring Break was a wonderful little break from school, except Auntie always seemed to be stomping around within hailing distance unless we were climbing the red rock cliffs. I can't prove it, but I suspect she is the one who kept crumbling up crackers and placing them in my bed between the sheets. For some reason, she blamed me because the parrot kept telling people that she was getting fat. She had not been able to train it to stop saying that. **BUT** she was able to teach it to say, "Peter wants crackers in his bed, Ho Ho Ho, Auntie's parrot said."

Auntie was a font (fountain) of unrequested information explaining such things as The Mistletoe Curse. She said except for a small window during the holidays, standing under the mistletoe did not give one permission to kiss. In fact, she declared, it was quite the opposite. It was a warning. She said, ignoring the Mistletoe Warning could cause certain parts of the male anatomy to fall off. And messing with the vocabulary of someone else's parrot could result in dire consequences.

Then there were the repeated warnings about nothing should interfere with Grace's graduating from Fort Lewis. Grace's parents were in complete agreement, probably because of Auntie's dire sermons and continuous lectures. Sarge and Grace's mom were starting to regard me as more of a problem than just a minor annoyance.

Auntie also mentioned, "Are you aware that someone with a telescope can see everything that happens on the red rocks?"

We hiked the hills, climbed the cliffs, and helped in the store. I even found an edition of "How the West Was Won" and finished it. My Indian friend Perry patted me on the back and said he was glad to see I was still hanging in there and that Sarge or Auntie hadn't shot me. Everyone else in the family was nice to me and kept telling me they were sooo glad Grace had found someone like me who was wise enough to wait before rushing into marriage.

Marriage? *Where did that come from?* I hadn't been thinking about getting married. I was happy with the status quo. And yes, I was definitely wise enough.

Drive to School

On the way back to campus I was feeling a little tired and sleepy after driving the thirty miles north to Gallup. I asked Grace if she would drive for a while. Maybe as far as Shiprock (90 miles).

I went right off to sleep in the first five miles. It couldn't have been over ten minutes or more after that when I started to wake up. I had the feeling something was wrong. The road wasn't as smooth as it should be, and the car seemed to be chugging. I opened my eyes and looked around to see what was the matter with the road and the car. Had Auntie poured sugar in my gas tank?

There was nothing wrong with the road. It was as smooth as a looking glass and devoid of most trucks and cars . . . including ours. I looked at our driver. She was asleep with a goofy-looking grin on her face.

The good news was her foot had slipped off the accelerator, and we were bumping along at a slowly decreasing speed. The bad news was we were headed towards a small ravine.

"WHOA! NELLIE!" I shouted.

It was more a comment than a command. WHOA may work with horses and girlfriends (sometimes), but it is not as effective on machinery. I jammed my foot on the brake and grabbed the steering wheel.

Within a fraction of a second (I repeat: within the fraction of **one** second) Grace awoke and her foot came slamming down on top of mine trying to force my gallant metatarsals to crash through the floorboard. The result was the car came to a complete stop with the speed of a champion roping horse, and I walked with a limp for the next three weeks. Her other foot slammed onto the clutch pedal, causing the engine to race.

She tried to wrestle the steering wheel from me. Her adrenalin gave her additional strength. As we fought she screamed, "What are you trying to do, kill us?"

"No, but I'm thinking about it."

As I said, the car came to a complete stop. I reached over and turned off the ignition as the dust settled. "You're fired as the driver," I declared.

Grace looked around, slowly calming down. I was sitting in the passenger's seat and she was behind the steering wheel. We were 30 feet from the highway and about 70 feet short of a small ravine. The true nature of the situation slowly dawned on her.

"I must have fallen asleep," she said. (That was in the days before seatbelts were made mandatory. My little car did not have any.) She spotted the ravine.

"OH OH. Good thing we stopped. That could have been . . . very . . . embarrassing," she said after searching for the perfect word. I didn't agree that "embarrassing" was the perfect word. *How about "dead" or "maimed" for life?* I thought.

"Yeah," I said, "St. Peter and the boys would have had a lot of laughs at our expense as they welcomed us in."

It was 15 years (1980 to be exact) before I ever asked her to share the driving on a long trip and 65 years (2030) before I ever went to sleep when she was driving. (That is my clever way of saying, it hasn't happened yet. I figure I'll be in my nineties then, and what the heck. On second thought, maybe 2040.)

Back on Campus

It was a wonderful time for me. I was not worried about grades because the trimester was just about over and I had been told I was passing in all my classes. However, I wasn't even close to straight A's this time. My grades would be mostly B's with an A or a C thrown in. I had been hired by a school district in California that had sent a representative through on a recruiting trip. They paid a thousand more than the highest Colorado school district. Being a male in a female-dominated job market (elementary school teacher) made me quite employable.

I had my own car, so I was mobile, and I had a girlfriend that had been with me for over seven months. Before Grace, I had never been able to keep one for over a month and the average time was about one date. On one memorable and record-breaking instance: five minutes into the first date. It might have had something to do with me asking the question, "How do you feel about Dutch Treat dates?" For the record, she was against them.

Grace had not done that well with her grades. She blamed me. She said she was either with me or thinking about me and not thinking about her classes. (She has always thought I was more desirable than I actually am. She still feels that way. I have been magnanimously willing to overlook this little fault in her judgment.)

I was okay with the idea of letting her finish her college before taking our relationship to the next level.

Then one day I got the wake-up call. I was waiting in the hall for Grace to get out of a class; she wasn't expecting me. (The professor in my class couldn't get his car started, and after 20 minutes without a teacher, everybody walked out.)

As the students came out of Grace's class there was a boy walking next to her. They were laughing and chatting about something that had happened in class. The hall was full of students and she didn't see me as she was giving him her full attention. I was jealous. The green-eyed monster took control of my body.

Friendly Henry put his hand on her shoulder. (Grr). She did not push it off, slap his face, or throw root beer on his lap like she had done to the obnoxious suitor when she worked at A & W as a carhop. (GRR, GRR, GRR)

I was outraged; I saw red, (in fact, I saw all the primary colors and a few of the secondary ones) but I didn't do anything . . . **then**. But the next time that class met two days later, I was in the hall waiting for them to come out. I had ditched my class and armed myself with a well-shaken can of root beer. Any laughing, flirting, or shoulder touching would bring forth an instant rainbow cascade of root beer.

When the class came out into the hall, Grace was walking and talking and smiling and laughing with . . . some girls. Shoulder touching "Hands" Romeo was talking with some guy about the Dodgers chances that season. I felt embarrassed, but it was not a complete loss. At least I still had my root beer. I popped the top intending to chugalug the whole thing and drown my embarrassment. I drowned more than my embarrassment. Root beer shot out of the can, all over me and anyone within 10 feet of me as I tried to avoid the sticky liquid spray.

I tried to explain to those around me. I said, "OOPS."

That explanation did not seem to satisfy everyone, or anyone. There was some talk about tar and feathering but it evaporated as the bell for the next class rang. The only ones left in the hall were Grace and me.

"What are you doing here?"

"I brought you a root beer," I said weakly and held out the mostly empty can.

That explanation went over about as well as the "OOPS" explanation. She had not gone unscathed. In fact, you might say she was scathed, scathed pretty good, a primary scathee.

"Thank you so much, but I prefer my root beer stirred, not shaken." (It was the year the first James Bond movie came out.)

Somehow she didn't sound sincere. That line about stirred not shaken sounded less contentious when Sean Connery said it.

The thing about the incident was it made me realize it would not be a good idea to leave her in this environment for three years with all sorts of shoulder touching Bozos hitting on her.

Grace, for her part, didn't like the idea of me being in California with money in my pocket as a freewheeling young bachelor 80 miles from Hollywood and 30 miles from Palm Springs.

The Decision

I don't remember having one real date until Jr. College. I mean the kind of date where you got over your fear of being rejected and phoned the girl and asked if she wanted to go to the movies or a dance with you.

Then things picked up. I was incredibly good looking according to my grandmother. I had finally grown and was 6'1." All the good men my age had already been snapped up, and no one knew what a dating dud I was in high school.

I don't actually remember proposing or being proposed to. I just remember we didn't want to risk losing each other or tempting fate. We also knew her family was against it and might try to stop it.

Neither one of us knew anything about getting married. I did remember seeing a movie on television many years earlier when I was in elementary school. The hero and his girlfriend showed up at the door of a kindly old Justice of the Peace and announced they wanted to be married.

The man turned and shouted to his wife who was in the kitchen doing the dishes, "Martha, come here, this nice young couple wants to get married, and we need a witness."

The next thing I remember about the movie was they were saying "I do" followed by the old gentleman saying they were married, the hero could kiss the bride, and the hero handing him $5.

I told Grace what I remembered and she said there must be more to it than that. I suggested we go see my old roommate Lyle (008). He had married Gwen and they were living off-campus.

Lyle answered the door. "Igor, my friend," he said as he opened the door. Igor is a name that conjures up images of The Hunchback of Notre Dame, and the assistant or butler to Dr. Frankenstein, or Count Dracula. He had called me that ever since a funny incident which happened in the student center the previous summer. I told Lyle all about the movie with the kindly Justice of the Peace and asked if there was anything else we needed to do.

He was shocked by my ignorance. "Was this movie in black and white?"

"Yes."

"Did it have sound or was there cards on the screen telling you what they said?"

"Sound."

I explained how we had to keep our intentions secret because her family would be against it, and try to stop us. I let him know that they were a real rough and tumble outfit in the mold of Louis L'Amour heros. Plus, there was a loony aunt that needed to be locked up and was scarier than any Igor or serial killer and would be only too happy to see me on my way in a hearse.

All this appealed to Lyle. He said he would help. The danger brought out the side of his personality that had found out the name of the girl who had loaned me the pencil by slipping into Dr. Smith's office when Dr. Smith was away.

Lyle said he would take charge and wrote a list of things for us to do. The first was to go to the county clerk and apply for a license. What he didn't mention, he probably forgot, there was a section in the local paper, the Durango Herald, which reported things like deaths, births, and *those getting married.*

I nearly wet my pants when Susan congratulated me on my upcoming nuptials.

"My what?" I quickly scanned my body for anything amiss or upcoming, especially in the area of where I thought my nuptials might dwell.

"Marriage," she said when she realized I had no idea what a nuptial was. I looked up relieved.

"WHO TALKED?" I shouted. "Was it Lyle? I'm gonna bust him in the nose. It was supposed to be a secret."

"Tisk-tisk It was in the paper," she said.

"GOOD LORD CRIED THE WOODCHUCK. That is about as far from keeping a secret as one can get. Was it on the radio and television too?"

"I have no idea," Susan said. "Have you got the results of your blood tests yet?"

"BLOOD TESTS! HELL NO!" This
was the first I heard anything about blood tests. There was no mention of blood tests in the movie. **"I have blood. Lots of blood. And it's going to stay right where it is. . . I don't need any test."**

"You tell them, Tiger," she said before hurrying away to pull the wings off butterflies.

Tiger told them and gave them his little speech. But it did absolutely no good. As the Latinos say, "No Bueno por nada."

Petrarch Grant Wheatley III

Isn't that a heck of a moniker? My real name is Peter Grant Wheatley. I had never really liked the name Peter although I was okay with "Pete."

I might have been okay with Peter if someone years earlier hadn't kept his wife in a pumpkin shell. And there is also that thing about equating the name with part of the human anatomy. When I got to Durango, I introduced myself as Pete Wheatley.

Grace wanted to know if the "Pete" was short for Peter. I told her "no" that it stood for something much worse. I told her it was an ugly name. I told her I was embarrassed to tell people. But she was relentless. Finally, I told her the "P" stood for Petrarch.[2] For a moment she stood in shocked silence. Then she said, "That is a lovely name." I could tell she was lying and didn't really like it.

As we were filling out the marriage forms I suddenly got hit in the back of the head. "What for you bop me in the head?"

"Well Peter, it's nice to know the correct name of the man I am going to marry. And it's nice to know it isn't Petrarch."

---

[2] Italian poet and scholar. Lived 1304-1374. Leader of the Italian Renaissance. Wrote many poems to Laura over forty years. She was the wife of another.

Wedding Day

Finally, all the bells, whistles, and head bopping had been accomplished. It was our wedding day. I was a nervous wreck. I hadn't slept more than a couple of hours. We had made plans to meet at 0800. I started watching the clock at 0300 and urging it to pick up speed. It was like the saying about a watched pot never boils. In those five hours, I must have aged five days. It beat all my childhood memories of my brother and I lying in bed on Christmas morning waiting for permission to get out of bed.

Then it happened. The clock said it was 0800. I was already dressed in my finest clothes. I was not in a suit because I didn't own a suit, but I was looking good. I looked out the window, she was not there.

I stood looking out the window for 15 minutes getting nervous and nervouser. *Had her parents arrived early to take her home? Had she changed her mind? Had her heart stopped because she was so excited about marrying me?*

At 0830 I went out and started throwing little pebbles at her window. At 0845 she came to the window. Thank goodness. My arm was getting tired, and I was running out of pebbles. She looked like she had just gotten out of bed. She claimed her alarm had not gone off. I was so relieved that was the reason, I shouted, "I'll meet you in the parking lot at ten and we will go to town for breakfast."

She made it by 1015. *She and I are going to have to have some serious talks on the subject of punctuality,* I thought to myself.

As she jogged down to the parking lot she passed a group of girls walking towards the student center. One named Sandy shouted, "Have a great summer Grace."

She called back, "Thank you. I'm getting married today." They cheered. One even gave her the *"way to go"* sign.. That girl's name was Mary.

After breakfast, we went over to Lyle and Gwen's to wait. Lyle said our appointment at the church was for 1300. He noticed there was a diffence of five minutes between his watch and mine and suggested we synchronize our watches.

Like I said, I was wearing my best clothes. I did not have a suit but I thought I looked pretty decent. Gwen just looked okay. Lyle was a fashion plate wearing an expensive suit and looking like a Mississippi gambler. Grace was stunning. She looked like a movie star.

Perhaps that is why the preacher kept trying to marry Grace to Lyle. A couple of times he addressed groom questions to Lyle instead of me. And he kept maneuvering Lyle and Grace together. I was starting to smell a rat, and I wondered if he was a real preacher.

"Do you Peter take this woman to be your natural wedded wife?"

"No."

"Why?"

"Because my name is Lyle."

"Do you Lyle take this woman . . ."

"No."

"Why?"

"I already have a wife."

I raised my hand for permission to speak. The preacher nodded at me, giving me permission. "My name is Peter, and I'll take this woman."

"Thank God," said the preacher. "The last thing we need around here is an extra wife." After a pause, he asked, "Peter, do you have a ring?"

"No."

"Oh dear. We need a ring."

It **really** confused the (?) preacher when Lyle took the ring off Gwen's finger and handed it to Grace. Grace slipped it on her finger to see if it would fit. Then Grace after a brief struggle managed to get it off, causing several of us to breathe a sigh of relief. She handed the ring to me, so I could give it back to her during the ceremony.

"Are you planning on marrying both of them . . . with the same ring?" he asked Grace.

She shook her head.

"Good. You can only have one at a time," he continued.

I left the church not quite sure whether I had been made a husband or a best man and if Lyle had been made a bigamist, or if Grace had two husbands. I feel the minister had the same problem and I was not sure he was a real preacher.

I gave him five dollars like in the movie. A shocked look crossed Lyle's face and the preacher's. He looked like he had been expecting more. As we were leaving the church, I think I spotted Lyle slipping the man a couple of twenties.

It crossed my mind that Lyle might have hired someone to impersonate a man of the cloth. If so, he hadn't picked a very good one. We were always playing jokes on each other. I hoped this wasn't one of those times.

I questioned Lyle on this in the parking lot. He said quote, "To the best of my knowledge, the guy was a real preacher." To me, that wasn't a 100% positive statement that the man was a real preacher. And Lyle sort of chuckled when he said it and didn't look me in the eyes. I didn't know whether to tell Grace of my suspicions or not. She seemed so happy. And if the guy wasn't legitimate, what could I do? I decided to keep quiet.

After the ceremony, we went over to Lyle's to change into more comfortable clothes for traveling. I remember saying as we walked into their house, "Grace, you can go into the bedroom and change first." She picked up a suitcase and started off.

Lyle and Gwen laughed and one of them gave me a shove and the other said, "You're married now. It's okay to look."

My face turned red, and I grabbed my backpack and followed Grace. We both entered the bedroom to change clothes for the trip and show Lyle and Gwen that we were big people now. However, we were both so shy that we faced in opposite directions and didn't peek. At least I didn't.

Before re-entering the living room I turned to the fully dressed Grace and said, "We may have a problem." I was going to tell her of my suspicions about the preacher Lyle had hired.

"You're telling me," she moaned. "I've been trying for the last half hour to get it off." She was still wearing Gwen's wedding ring. The earlier struggle to get it off must have caused her finger to swell.

"I guess we will just have to tell them we will mail it back to them when your finger returns to normal size."

"I don't think that is going to work."

Gwen was not a happy camper. For 20 minutes and half a bottle of dishwashing detergent, the ring refused to leave Grace's finger. With each minute, Gwen became more upset. At the end of 20 minutes, Gwen suggested we cut it off.

"It will be a shame to ruin such a pretty ring," I said.

"No, I'm talking about the finger. We can take her up to the hospital and get it reattached."

Grace managed to get the ring off before Gwen returned from the kitchen carrying a large . . . cup of coffee . . . AND . . . more dishwashing soap and a jar of Vaseline. SUCCESS.

About four o'clock the **E**loping **T**wosome crowded into the little car nicknamed Minnie Mouse and headed east. They were happy yet worried that something might still happen to spoil their happiness. The plan was to drive as far as the next town or two before phoning home. I'll let Pete tell you in his own words.

Honeymoon Motel

Grace looked at the map and suggested we stop in Pagosa Springs. She thought it sounded romantic and calming. Much more so than South Fork, Del Norte, or Alamosa. And those towns were on the other side of a high, steep, mountain pass with the scary name Wolf Creek.

As we headed into Pagosa Springs, I was nervous. I had never checked into a motel with a woman. I knew they checked car licenses. Did they also need to see a marriage license? That hadn't been mentioned in the movie.

I blame my ignorance on my parents. They must have been drinking or on drugs the night I was conceived, and when they checked into a motel on family trips they made Alan and I wait in the car.

The name of the motel was the Harvey House and it looked quite respectable. Grace said she would wait in the car while I checked in. What a rotten thing to do to me. We were both feeling a little self-conscious. To be perfectly honest as opposed to mostly honest, I had been planning on asking her to check in while I checked the oil and the fluid in the radiator.

I couldn't admit to my bride that I was nervous and a little bit Rhode Island Red.[3] I walked into the lobby and told the man that I would like a room for me and my girl fr-. . . my wife. My face reddened. I forced my voice to be lower than normal and I tried to look casual. He looked at me suspiciously.

I boldly told him the number on the license plate. He didn't move or say anything. He just stood there studying me. I put my driver's license on the counter, followed by my marriage certificate, birth certificate, and my diploma from Fort Lewis. NOTHING. I offered to let him phone my old roommate Lyle or my counselor at Fort Lewis, Nick Heidy if he needed references. I warned him that if he phoned Lyle and a woman answered, to hang up. (Gwen was still fuming and claiming Grace had stretched her wedding ring because it kept slipping off her finger.)

---

[3] Chicken

I think he was about to suggest I move on to Kooksville, South Fork, Monte Vista, Del Norte or Alamosa when Grace came in. She was wondering what was taking so long. People like Grace. While she was visiting with him I started scooping up my proof of identity and preparing to head on to the next town, not Kooksville. The man asked Grace what had happened to her finger. And of course, she told him the whole story. That woman would chat with a fire hydrant or a parking meter.

When Grace had finished, the man behind the desk announced, "Mr. and Mrs. Wheatley, I'd like to welcome you to the Harvey House." (I looked around for my parents. In my mind, **they** were Mr. and Mrs. Wheatley. I was Pete and Grace was Grace.)

The man continued, "**Mr. Wheatley,** I would like to offer you the Honeymoon Suite at no extra cost." As he handed Grace the key he whispered, "I think you could have done better."

"I wonder what the Honeymoon Suite is like," Grace said as we walked out. "Wasn't that nice of Harold to give us an upgrade?"

"HAROLD," I said loud enough for him to hear. "Are we now on first-name basis with the help?"

All the apartments were the same. Harold was just being a smart ass.

No, I am wrong. One of the apartments that night **was** the Honeymoon Suite. The lovemaking was good, but the best part was falling asleep and waking up in the arms of someone who loved me as much as I loved her. It's been well over fifty years (closer to sixty) since that night, and I still get that same feeling every morning when I wake up next to her, and I thank the Lord for **our** Grace (HIS and mine).

E. T. Phone Home

We, the Eloping Twosome, phoned the ranch the next day from Pagosa Springs figuring the extra 60 miles from Durango and additional twelve hours overnight wouldn't hurt the chances for my survival. Her mother answered.

"Hi," I said. "Guess who this is."

"Telemarketer."

"No. This is your favorite son-in-law." (Was that cool?)

"Don't have one. I only have one daughter and she'd have to be married for me to even have one son-in-law and they are going to wait until she grad-u-a . . . Oh God! NO!"

Then there was total, stunned silence as her brain tuned into the true picture. The silence might have lasted a minute, but it seemed much longer. Finally, she said, "OH NO, YOU AREN'T CONTEMPLATING . . . !" Then there was another minute of semi-silence. I felt the need to say something.

I broke the silence by saying, "I HAVE CONTEMPLATED. The contemplating is over."

More silence. Well, not exactly silence. She was holding her hand over the mouthpiece and talking to someone else in the room. I could only make out a couple of the words which sounded like "get," "gun," and "kill."

Then she came back on the line and asked in a super sweet voice, "Where are you, favorite son-in-law?"

"The Harvey House Motel," said I. I knew the second that was out of my mouth that I might have made a terrible blunder.

She was hot on the trail now. "And where is that my beloved, favorite, wonderful, son-in-law?" I was not falling for this super nice voice a second time. I wondered if she could call the police and have us held 'til they arrived. Suddenly Pagosa did not seem far enough away. I did not reveal the real name of the town. In fact, I might have let it slip that we were in Las Vegas, NV which is 180 degrees in the opposite direction and 600 miles from where we were. (Did I mention that after math, geography is one of my worst areas of expertise?)

That was when Grace took over the phone, and I packed us up, loaded the car and started warming it up for a quick getaway. After an hour, Grace got her mother calmed down. I kept trying to get Grace to hang up thinking they were having the call traced.

I learned later the sarge was so happy he went out and sat on the wall and wouldn't talk to anyone for three hours. He just sat there cleaning his shotgun and singing, "Hang down your head Tom Dooley" but substituting the name Pete Wheatley for Tom's name. This was not only rude but hypocritical because approximately 30 years earlier he and Donna had done the very same thing.

The reaction was a little different when I phoned home. The phone was answered by Mom.

"Hi Mom, guess who this is."

"Can you give me a hint?" I heard a click and knew Dad had picked up the extension.

"I got married."

"GOOD! Now you are someone else's responsibility," chuckled Dad.

"Why didn't you do it last week when we were down there for your graduation?" Mom asked.

Dad: "What are your plans for the summer?"

Me: "Spend one month at Camp Pendleton and then maybe spend the rest of the summer with you guys."

Mom: "I am not a guy."

Dad: "I don't think so, Pete. This apartment isn't big enough for the both of . . . uh two couples. I'll give you **ten** days to find something. Thanks for the call." CLICK

Mom: Your dad is such a kidder. Thank you for the call.

I had not got the impression that the Great Kidder was great kidding.

After the initial shock wore off, both sets of parents were supportive and Grace's parents super supportive.

We had a week before, I had to report to Camp Pendleton for a month and Grace went home to Cousins Valley to face the music.

Alan phoned during that too-short week. He was excited about his impending marriage to Carolyn. When it was my turn to talk to him he asked if I was going to come up with Mom and Dad to his wedding like I had done for his graduation from Whitman.

"No."

"WHY?" said he.

"Because you didn't come to mine."

"WHAT? WHY? WOW? HOW? That's a shocker!" he gasped.

"Would you like to talk to her?" I offered.

"Yes!" I handed the phone to Grace. "Hello Alan," she said.

"Mary, welcome to the family."

I saw a shudder run through Grace's body, but you couldn't tell by her voice. "Thank you, **Alvin**," she said sweetly. "I grew up an only child and have always wanted a brother. Now that we're family, you can call me **Grace**. Bye." She handed the phone back to me and I handed it to Mom.

Mom kind of chuckled, winked at me, and said into the phone, "You kind of put your foot in your mouth, didn't you, **Alvin**?" Then she took the phone, which was on a long cord, into the bedroom.

Grace felt badly and wanted to apologize before they hung up, but I wouldn't let her. I told her when Alan was little, Mom used to call him "Sticky Drippin" and sing songs about today is the day they give babies away with a ten cents bar of soap. We went up to the top floor and enjoyed the lights of Denver as we hugged each other.

Even though Grace wasn't Mom's first choice for me, it was Grace who put her life on hold for the last two years of Mom's life. She cooked for her, cleaned up after her, and treated her super kindly and with great respect even as the dementia got worse. And it was Grace who rode in the back of the van with her holding her hand, where Mom lay on the mattress in pain on a midnight run to the emergency room thirty miles away. And it was Grace that cried by her bedside when she left us after 91 years of a life well-lived in March of 2005.

The Flight

As I said, we stayed with my folks for a little over a week until it was time for me to report to the Marines at Camp Pendleton. I caught a plane for San Diego and Grace boarded a plane for Gallup the same day. My plane made its destination, hers did not.

It was dark outside as Grace finally boarded three hours late. The plane scheduled for the flight had needed some minor tweaking or an attitude adjustment. Grace pulled the plastic curtain down which covered the inside of the window.

They were somewhere over the mountains when a couple in the seats in front of Grace said, "It looks like that engine is on fire." This piqued her curiosity. Grace lifted the blind and looked out. Yep, that engine was definitely on fire. It was blazing along merrily. She remembers wondering if that would cause the wing to melt and fall off.

"Don't you think we should tell someone?" she suggested.

The man across the aisle was looking out the window. "How is your side looking?" she asked. He gave her the thumbs-up sign. She turned to look out her window again and was shocked by how close to the ground they were. She gave the man the thumb-down sign. Grace was wishing she was sitting on the other side when suddenly the nose of the plane dropped, followed by the rest of the plane. Somewhere up front, a woman screamed.

Another called out, "Oh stewardess, I have changed my mind about not wanting an alcoholic beverage." Her friend from the safe side had assumed the crash position. The flight attendant was absolutely no help. She was sitting down, belted in, and doing something with some beads.

BUMP.

"What's that?" someone called out.

"We have either run into something like a flying duck, a tree top, or a mountain," someone answered. It turned out to be the lowering of the landing gear. A minute later the plane had made a successful emergency landing.

The flight attendant announced, "Take everything with you because you won't be flying any farther in this @#$%&* plane." I have it on good authority that Rachel's career in the air ended that night. She was heard to mutter something about applying for a job at Safeway when she got back to Phoenix. When they got to the terminal they saw that their luggage had beat them there.

They were told that the company was trying to find an available plane somewhere to help the passengers reach their destination, but it might take hours.

Grace phoned home. The sarge answered, listened, and then told Grace, "Don't move, I'm on the way. Here's your mother."

"Daddy, you don't have to do that."

"Too late," the mother said. "He just drove out the driveway."

The new Mrs. Wheatley and the sarge arrived at the ranch just before the sun came up.

Denver Summer

I got back to Denver from the Marines, and Grace from Gallup at the end of the month. We were both excited to be back together, and we both had exciting news to tell the other. "You first," she said

"I'm a PFC," I said proudly pushing out my chest.

"What's that? Is it curable?" She looked worried.

"It is not a virus. I did not say **I have** PFC, I said **I am** a P F C."

"WELL WHOOP DEE DOO AND RING OUT THE NEWS," she said facetiously "May I buy a vowel?"

"You are taking all the fun out of my big announcement. Becoming a PFC is a raise in pay, rank, and importance."

"Is it higher than a captain?"

"No."

"Is it higher than Sergeant? Can you tell Daddy to do things?" (For those not familiar with military rank, a PFC is the next to the lowest rank.)

"No."

"Who can you boss around? Is it higher than . . . anything?"

"Privates."

"Pirates? Did you say pirates? What on earth are you doing with pirates? Can you tell Auntie what to do?"

(I gave up. She had completely ruined my big announcement.) "What's **your** big news?" (I was ready to knock whatever little thing she had done out of the ballpark. I honed myself to make fun of whatever she said.")

"Are you R-E-A-D-Y?" she spelled.

I was starting to get tired of this spelling thing. From now on it would be words only from me. "I am ready. I am now a Private First Class, and I can handle anything you can spell." (You may have noticed I did not spell out the initials of my new rank this time.)

"We're going to have a B-A-B-Y" she spelled.

I sounded it out. "What is a Baa-bi? a Baab-eye? Bay-bi? a Bay-bee? . . . a BABY!!!"

I had to sit down before I fainted. I almost made it.

I didn't know how we were going to pay for it, but that was the greatest, happiest surprise I had ever had. It flew by me surpassing making Private First Class a nothing accomplishment. I was going to be a Daddy: a Daddy First Class, a DFC, a D-A-D-D-Y!

What were we going to do until school started? That would be almost another three months. I thought we could stay and mooch off my parents. They had different ideas. They said the apartment was too small for two families and invited us to find someplace else to squat. Dad reminded me that we only had eight days left before he started pitching my things over the balcony into the parking lot. And he suggested, that if we wanted to eat, we might like to find employment.

(I wish our government had this philosophy. If I hadn't been forced out of the nest, I would gladly have coasted all summer instead of being productive. I believe it is called tough love. At the time, however, I didn't appreciate tough love. I was wanting cotton candy love.)

We found a large two-story house several blocks away with a "Room for Rent" sign out front. The owner had turned it into a series of apartments. Our apartment consisted of two rooms. We had a kitchen, and we had a multi-purpose everything-else room. The bed fit into a large cabinet during the day. I think I heard someone call it a Murphy Bed.

I bet you have noticed something missing. If you haven't, you better get some Metamucil. It was up a flight of stairs, down the hall, and worked on a first-come first-serve basis.

My next problem was how was I going to pay for all this luxury? It would be three months before my teaching job would start. No Denver employers seemed impressed with the fact that after seven years I was finally a college graduate. One employer said as far as he was concerned, my degree and fifty cents would get me a good cup of coffee. I told him I was going to have a baby. He said, "See Rumpelstiltskin." The next day I went to the Manpower offices. The rules there were show up, work hard, and get minimum wage if chosen. (They charged the companies we worked for much more.)

We were busy. There had been some flooding by the South Platte and warehouse basements needed to be mucked out and cleaned before mold set in. There were also boxcars that needed to be unloaded. I impressed McMurtry Paint Company with how hard I worked and they told me to come back in two weeks and put in an application. I guess there was some rule against hiring Manpower workers within two weeks. I went back in two weeks and my salary tripled, plus I wasn't competing for a job every morning.

Grace got a job as a phone solicitor for an insurance company. She was good and the solicitors got a flat salary plus a percentage of the commission on any sales coming in from the appointments they had set up.

We were not in high cotton but we were in cotton. Let's call it middle cotton. We started buying things like food, clothes, and things that tickled our fancy. It was during this period, I saw an ad in the Denver Post's classified section. Some farmer in Longmont had Boxer puppies for sale. My best buddy growing up was my dog Flash, a Boxer. My son or daughter would need a dog. We named the new puppy Petrarch. We had to sneak the puppy in and out because the tenants weren't supposed to have pets.

My folks had been a little put out because they had come down for my graduation and even had dinner with us on the night before I graduated, but we did not let them in on our plans to get married in two days, going along with the idea that loose lips sink ships. Mainly it was my mom who was upset, I don't think my dad cared a wit and was probably grateful he didn't have to attend two weddings: both Alan's and mine.

It was nearly one wedding. It was the first time Grace met my parents. We were to meet at the Chief restaurant, one of my favorite places to eat in Durango. The reservations were for 5:00 p.m. They were on time, we were not. Grace had taken extra time getting ready and was nervous about the prospect of meeting her future parents-in-law, especially Dad. She had heard lots of stories about him.

When they got to Durango, Dad had his own private Happy Hour in the motel. Mom became the designated driver. When we were late, Dad went ahead and ordered. I can't remember what main dish he ordered but he ordered a side dish of spaghetti.

When we entered the restaurant we could hear someone yelling at a waiter. I recognized the voice and my heart sunk into my ankles. I hoped Grace wouldn't run for the hills. "WHAT KIND OF PLACE SERVES SPAGHETTI WITH OUT SAUCE?" the customer was shouting. They brought Dad a full plate of spaghetti with extra sauce. What Dad had done was take the small side dish of spaghetti and flip it onto his main dish, thus putting the sauce on the bottom and covered by the noodles. Only the whites of the noodles had been showing.

One time before we left Denver for California, Mom took Grace out to eat at the fanciest restaurant in the city. They were both dressed to the nines. Mom ordered Mediterranean Shrimp Kabobs with orange spinach and a white Chablis. Her new daughter-in-law ordered a Pepsi, cheeseburger, and fries. I don't know who was more shocked: the fancy waiter or Mom. I thought we were going to have to go into the witness protection program when I heard about the incident.

. . . .

Growing up, I caused Mom a lot of heartache and pain, but in all those years I never saw such a look of horror cross her face as the night we were invited over for dinner on my 26th birthday. The steak had been barbequed to perfection. Before even tasting it, Grace put catsup on her steak, before even taking one bite. I do not particularly like steak, . . .but it horrified me also. The evening became very uncomfortable after that and we left as soon as we could gracefully make our exit.

As we climbed into bed that night, I told Grace, "This may be my most unfavorite birthday of all."

She said, "It isn't over yet. I know something that might make it your favorite."

"What? You've decided to give up catsup?"

"No."

She was right. Just remembering that night has pushed the one when I got my first bicycle out of first place. And that was when I got a used Schwinn with coaster brakes and fat (balloon) tires which extended my sphere of influence from one block to the whole town of Montrose, California. I was ten.

. . . .

I believe Mom would have preferred me to marry someone more high-societal, and less naïve. I believe, actually, Mom would have preferred me to do a lot of things differently.

On Top of Spaghetti

I promise, this is my last mention of spaghetti. Mother and Dad considered themselves gourmets and for all I know, they probably were. I am not.

Growing up, a spaghetti dinner, our favorite, never came as a surprise because Mom started working on the sauce a day in advance. It would be simmering on the stove for hours. She would dip a spoon into the sauce, take a taste, and add a pinch of this or a pinch of that, depending on what she thought it needed. I don't remember what she was pinching. I just remember the house smelling wonderful.

Then on the next day, the spaghetti was served with garlic bread on sourdough French, an Italian salad, and with a proper drink like, Merlot, Zinfandel, or milk. (Hey, I was a kid.)

It was usually served by candlelight. The bottle the candle had been stuck in had been with us several years and the drippings clung to the outside of the bottle. It had all the colors of the rainbow and more.

We were taught how to stick our fork in and come out with a combination of sauce and noodles by twisting until it was all on the fork. Then we'd put the combination in our mouths and extract the fork. If any slipped off the fork or out of our mouth we were allowed to suck it in. The sucking it in was a fun part of eating spaghetti for Alan and me. Then came chewing the spaghetti and enjoying all the nuances of the sauce.

One Saturday Grace and I were invited over for a spaghetti dinner. It was all there, just the way I remembered from my childhood.

When the dinner was served, Dad said "Let's eat." At the speed of light Grace had hers cut up into bite-size squares. It reminded me of a mother with several little children cutting up the food for them. Dad couldn't believe his eyes which seemed to double in size and bug out. "AAGH," came voluntarily out of his throat. "Oh my," said Mother as though she had just witnessed a terrible traffic accident.

"This is really good," said Grace.

I've lost my appetite," said Dad. "I may never get it back."

It was a short "never." Mom said as soon as we left, it returned.

I asked Grace how they had done spaghetti when she was growing up.

She said, "Open the can, heat it up and eat it up.

Hilpert's Pants

Three years earlier when I was attending the University of Alaska, Dr. Hilpert was faced with the problem of rowdiness in the temporary dorm he had been put in charge of. The college had rented a CBQ[4] on the base from the army because all the dorms on campus were full. The students placed under his care were age-wise twenty-one and above. Many had served in Korea. They were not about to be bullied into accepting the same rules as were mandated for 18-year-old high school graduates.

The graduate student who had been assigned to him quit in terror when threatened with some type of torture or fragging. Doc offered me the job.

I said "NO! POSITIVELY NOT!!! NEVER!!! A MILLION TIMES NO!!!

He said, It comes with FREE room and board." I said, "I'll give it a **shot**." He said he hoped that wouldn't be necessary.

---

[4] Civilian Barracks Quarters

My approach was different than the graduate student. If a bunch of the guys were getting too noisy and drinking, I would enter the room waving a white flag and work on their love for the Doc who we called "Daddy John" because sometimes he reminded us of an old mother hen the way he fussed over and cared for us. I would say something like, "It's getting a little loud in here fellas. You don't want to get Daddy John in trouble with the college or the military police." Then I'd leave. The noise would usually cut down. They would police themselves.

One day Daddy John was not feeling well, and he sent me to a meeting representing our dorm. He told me to wear a suit. I told him I didn't have one. He went to his closet and came back with one made of the finest material. "Don't sit on any gum," he said with a smile handing it to me. I was super careful. When I tried to return the suit, he wouldn't take it. He said, "I might need you to represent this gang of hooligans again. At the college or in court," he said cracking a joke. The next time I tried to return it, he said he didn't wear second-hand clothes. "The suit is yours now." During my 2 years in Fairbanks, he was my best friend.

I have told all the above to explain any reference to Hilpert's pants. My wife got into Hilpert's pants.

It was a week after Grace made the announcement about the baby that Mom took Grace aside and told her that she wouldn't always be so trim and thin. She took Grace down to the basement in the apartment where the storage cages were located and started looking for material to make some maternity clothes. One of the things Grace spotted was my beautiful suit. Grace thought it would look good and professional on me when I was teaching school and threw it in the box Mom was putting material in. That afternoon they started making clothes using patterns from Simplicity.

I bet you have heard of Jack the Ripper, we had Jean the Seam Ripper. Grace was out of the room when Mom came across my suit. She attacked savagely with the seam ripper. Hilpert's pants became Grace's maternity dress for special occasions.

Window Washy

Pete's room

Climbing the walls

First Date Halftime

Private Wheatley

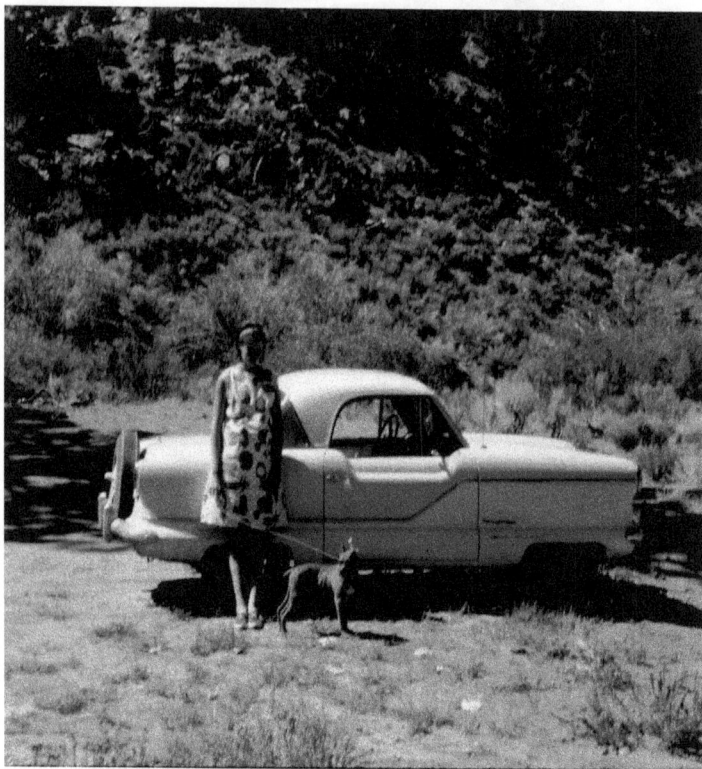

Rest stop: Big Bear to Pioneer Town

BOOK TWO

California

California or Bust

There was not a spare inch of space in Minnie Mouse when we left Denver. Our first stop would be the ranch. I wasn't sure that Minnie's suspension would hold up. The only place we could find for the puppy was in the glove compartment. Just kidding. We took the road south to Albuquerque and west to Gallup. I was afraid it wouldn't make it over the high Colorado mountain passes even if we chanted "I think I can, I think I can" and Grace got out and pushed.

I was planning on renting a little U-Haul trailer when we got to Gallup. When we got to Gallup we got a wonderful surprise. The sarge had a buddy named Chick who owned a used car lot, and Chick loaned us a station wagon to get our stuff out to California. Chick only asked we return it at the first opportunity.

The car was old and the tires looked to be on their last legs, but it made it possible for us to arrive in California with some possessions. The engine ran well as did the air conditioner, and this was important because we were heading into the Mojave Desert in August.

Everything went okay until halfway between Amboy (Not to be confused with OH BOY) and 29 Palms; we got a flat. The retread had decided this desert driving was not its cup of tea. I put the spare on which looked less dependable than the tire I had taken off. We were halfway between the two towns, so it made just as much sense to keep going as turn back.

It was pretty scary knowing that if anything else happened to the car, we would be alone and miles away from civilization. What if no one came along? (We hadn't seen many cars since we turned off I-40. Even worse, what if someone or someones stopped and they were the bad guys. I was prepared to fight to the death for my family but was anxious to prevent that being necessary. I cut the speed to 45 and nursed it the rest of the way. We eventually came into Twenty-Nine Palms on a wing and a prayer. I would have said pins and needles, but I steered around anything that looked like a pin or a needle. We checked into a motel. We would contact the school district in the morning after buying a tire.

The next morning, we were grateful to be alive, but not too pleased with my choice of school districts. We had spent the last year mostly in beautiful green Colorado. Hardly anything was green here and any vegetation was covered with stickers and thorns.

"Nice looking sand," Grace said. I couldn't tell if she was trying to be nice or funny. I chose not to respond. I was getting the hang of the husband's role in this marriage thing.

We drove around until we found a service station that had the tire we needed. In New Mexico, I could have bought two tires, maybe three, for what they charged me.

"They are mighty proud of their tires out here in the desert," Grace commented as we left the service station. I couldn't tell if she was trying to be nice or funny. I chose not to respond.

We drove to the district offices so I could pick up my assignment and go over and check out my school. I was told I had not reached my final destination yet. I still had 20 miles to go to a place called Yucca Valley. "You'll love it," they said.

I couldn't tell if they were trying to be nice or funny. I chose not to respond. I got the impression they were "yuk-ing" and "valleying" it up at my expense.

I remembered something I'd heard when I was at 29 Palms with the Denver unit: "This isn't Hell, but you can see it from here."

I told Grace we still had another 20 miles to go. "Such a long trip," she said with a smile, "We're almost there. I can almost see it from here." I did not find that comforting.

We went back to the motel to load up. I had been planning on staying there until I found a place to rent in 29 Palms.

If 29 Palms, the head of the school district, looked like someplace I didn't want to live, what would this Yucca Valley be like? I'd probably be teaching all grades in a one-room school house and maybe living in it too.

Yucca Valley

Yucca Valley was almost like Camelot. There were more businesses than 29 Palms and everything seemed friendlier. Well, not really like Camelot. We still hadn't seen any green grass or knights jousting.

We had been told there was a member of the school board named Purcell who was a realtor that lived in Yucca Valley. We phoned and made an appointment to see him after lunch and then went exploring.

There were lots of nice houses, and we found the school. It looked great. There were many permanent school buildings and one under construction or was it destruction. It was in three pieces and reminded me of a building that some unhappy student had dynamited.

"I hope that isn't going to be a classroom." The temporary building was apart from all the rest of the buildings, and I mean APART. The only humans around the school were the school's two janitors who were getting everything ready for the next week.

We walked in through the main gate and in front of the main office was a large square with a flagpole in the middle. I would say the square was 20X 20 feet and it had been planted in grass. Beautiful green thick grass. We ran back to the car and grabbed our most recent purchases: pop, bread, mayonnaise, catsup, chips, and baloney; we had a picnic.

One of the janitors came over and wanted to know what we were doing there. I told him I was one of the new teachers, and we were having a picnic. He didn't look happy about the situation but said he guessed it would be all right if we didn't leave a mess and warned us the principal was very particular about appearances.

The man (me) and his wife (Grace) and little puppy (Petrarch Poopsy) were sitting in the square on the grass having a wonderful time when the principal arrived. He mistook us for some homeless indigents. He probably thought we were living in the old station wagon he had seen in the parking lot. The one with the one good tire and three bald ones.

After coughing three times to get our attention, he informed us he was the principal, this was a school, not a public park, and we were to vacate the premises immediately.

I looked at my watch, it was nearly time to meet with the school board member. We left without revealing who we were. I hoped he wouldn't recognize me when I reported for duty the following week. I thought of growing a beard but there wasn't enough time. Any attempt would just make me look like a little boy with a dirty face. One thing I could do was get a short haircut. I had not had a haircut since starting to work in Denver. I hoped a flattop or a butch would make me look like a different person.

"They told me they were teachers." I looked back. It was the janitor I had talked to. He was trying to explain to the principal why he had let us stay.

The principal ordered the janitor to lock the gate before any more gypsies or tramps came in. He looked up at the temporary building and shook his head. "I don't see how we can have Wheatley's classroom ready by next week." (I felt like a dagger had been jammed into my heart. I must have flooded the car.) At first, it didn't look like the car would start, but I kept cranking. Then it gave in to my persistence with a loud backfire and a thick puff of smoke.

It had never done that before or after when it was with us. I'm thinking it might have had something to do with the engine being adjusted for a much higher elevation. Unfortunately, the principal and the janitor had come over to see what the holdup (delay) was. They were in the line of fire from the exhaust pipe. Fortunately, the janitor took the brunt. I dropped it in gear and we left post haste (pealed out).

I told Grace not to feel badly, even Camelot had some stinkers. She asked me if I was fired. I did not have a good answer, so I said, "I have it on good authority that we will not be invited to his birthday party this year."

My sense of humor vibrates at a higher level than hers and she stayed on subject.

"Did you get the doggie pooh picked up?" she asked. "It would be terrible if he stepped in it."

"I have it on good authority that our exclusion also extends to Petrarch." She didn't laugh.

"I think Petrarch must be allergic to pickles and peanut butter," she said. He had got ahold of one of my sandwiches when my attention was diverted.

I interrupted her. "Grace, quit asking so many questions." I was thinking how this situation was like the movie Mr. Roberts where things kept happening to the Captain's palm tree. I was afraid if they made a movie of my life, I would come across more like Ensign Pulver than Mr. Roberts.

Angel One

Robert Purcell was sitting at a desk studying some papers and smoking a pipe. He was nearly the size of Eric (The Derrick) Meany, but nice. He offered us chairs. Once we were seated he started asking me questions to determine our needs. His voice sounded familiar. (It turns out that when I was a teenager living in the Los Angeles Basin he was the president of KFWB Los Angeles' most popular radio station.) He retired about the same time we moved to Alaska.

Robert (Call me Bob) quickly learned everything about us except I didn't like chopped liver. (A guy has to have some secrets). He learned I had just graduated and my wallet was nearly running on empty, nothing but fumes. Near the end of the interview, I asked him if the school district had any rules about the teachers having a second job, and Grace said she would be looking for work too.

That was the first time she had spoken other than to say, "Hi, my name is Grace and I'm pleased to meet you," when we were introducing ourselves.

"You've been mighty quiet, young lady, I mean Grace. Is there anything else you'd like to tell me?"

She hesitated. I prayed with all my heart that she wouldn't start talking. My prayers were not answered. Grace blurted out, making it sound like we were Bonnie and Clyde and had just robbed the Yucca Valley bank, "We got kicked out of the school yard for having a picnic on the grass."

The big man smiled.

"And Petrarch pooped on it."

I groaned.

The big man laughed, and said, "I see Marvin's on the job. He is a good principal but he does love that square of grass. Anything else, Grace?"

"No," I said forcibly. I was glaring at her trying to will her to shut up.

"Yes!" She smiled and said proudly, "We are going to have a baby."

I slapped my forehead and let out another groan. I was thinking, *I should have left you in the car with the puppy.* Petrarch was tied to the front bumper and resting comfortably in the shade of the car.

"Anything else, Grace?"

"No," said I.

"Yes," said Grace. "We have a dog."

The big man smiled. I could tell he was enjoying my discomfort. "I'm a cat man myself. I have two great Siamese, Ding Ding and Ling Ling. Anything else, Grace?"

I finally caught Mrs. Blabbermouth's attention by waving my hands in front of her face and giving her a stern look and the hush sign (index finger in front of the lips). "No, nothing else," she said.

"I've got a few ideas I'd like to kick around," he said. "Can you come back tomorrow? Say about eleven o'clock? Where are you staying while you are looking for a more permanent place?"

"That's the next thing on our list," I said.

Bob had the good manners not to ask if we had a price range or ask what we could afford. He had pretty well figured that out from his questions. "I've got a good idea," he said. "I have a friend named Ken who owns a motel and barbershop east of town. Let me give him a call and see if he has a vacancy."

He went to another room to make the call. He talked softly, but he had the kind of voice that penetrates. He was telling Ken about our situation and guaranteeing the bill if we couldn't pay.

Ken and his wife, whose name I can't remember, treated us royally. For the next three years that we lived in Yucca Valley, I always got my haircuts there and anyone that visited us, we recommended their motel if the visitors weren't insisting on a motel with a swimming pool. When Mr. Purcell found us a place and we moved out, the bill was exactly half of what they normally charged.

House on the Hill

It was called Yucca Valley because it was surrounded by hills and there were lots of Yuccas. On one side of the valley was Desert Christ Park with 12 foot statues portraying different scenes from the Bible. Above the park, on the hill overlooking the valley, were several houses.

We were riding with Bob in his jeep as he drove us around showing us several places that were out of our price range. We had just passed Desert Christ Park when he down shifted, turned the wheel to the right, and took a path straight up the side of the mountain. We didn't stop until he turned into the yard of the 2nd house from the top.

"What do you think of that view?" Bob asked.

"Awesome," said Grace.

I opened my eyes. "Okay if you're an eagle," said I.

We could see nearly everything in the valley. It made one feel like a king.

"Come, let's look inside. I've got the key. The house was empty. The kitchen had a stove, refrigerator, and a sink with a large window that looked out over the valley. There were also two bedrooms and a bathroom. Behind the house was a large water tank.

"Who could afford this place," I asked, "Elvis?"

"It belongs to a friend of mine who lives in the valley. He bought it as an investment but then he got sick before it was finished. He told me that he couldn't afford to pay anything, but he would feel more comfortable if there was someone trustworthy to housesit for a couple of months. Would you be interested?"

"NO. I'm sorry, Bob. I am going to have to say NO. My usual price for housesitting is one thousand a month, but now that I am married I would have to charge two thousand."

That must not have been the reaction he had been expecting. His mouth dropped open, and stayed that way.

"Are you out of your cotton-picking mind?" That was my bride. She never talked to me that way when she was courting me. I thought of one of the signs I had seen on the wall of a warehouse I was cleaning last summer. It read, "BEATINGS WILL CONTINUE UNTIL MORALE IMPROVES."

Bob was the first to catch on that I was joking. He gave me a pat of appreciation on the back that sent me staggering across the kitchen floor. Grace gave me the silent treatment for eight and a half minutes, a record for the Jabberwocky.

I was afraid that the station wagon would not make it up the steep incline, but somehow it made it, most of the time. There were a few times when we had to back down and get a better run at it.

What a wonderful place this Yucca Valley is turning out to be, I thought. *We have been here two days and we have free rent for a couple of months in a house on top of the mountain . . . well almost the top.*

A couple of days later Bob showed up and suggested we go to Harold's and thank him for the use of his house. When we got to Harold's it looked like he was having a party. It turned out to be a party for us. People were contributing things like couches, beds, chairs, etc. And men with trucks offered to deliver them to the house on the hill.

When the sun went down that night we had a furnished house with one of the best views in Yucca Valley. The furnishing included some lawn furniture, and we sat together looking at our kingdom as the sun went down. When it got dark we saw a movie come on at the drive-in theater. The picture was clear and close enough to see, but we had no sound. *"I'll have to talk to our resident angel about that."* I said, or *learn to read lips.*

Yucca Valley Elementary

I was a little nervous when I headed to the school for the first day. There would be a couple of days of last-minute preparing and then the students would come. I was nervous because of the picnic on the grass incident. I got out of the car half a block away thinking "someone" might recognize the car that had disrespected a principal and a janitor. I looked different.

I had Ken give me a short flattop, and I wore nice clothes, not the kind tourists wear for comfort when traveling . . . or picnicking. The other teachers were dressed more casual because it would be a work day getting their classrooms ready.

During the first faculty meeting, the principal kept looking at me. Finally, he asked, "Have we met before? You look so familiar."

(I don't remember exactly what I told him. I dropped into my Peter the Prevaricator mode.)

"You look so familiar," he repeated. "Do you know what a doppelganger is?"

"Two gangers," I guessed. I could not tell if I had fooled him or not.

A bell rang and the meeting started. One of the items near the end of the agenda was respecting the square in front of the office and not walking on the grass. I think it was Number 30 on the list.

Then he told us a story about a group of hippies that had squatted on the holy ground, desecrating it. He said the band of vagabond had herds of sick animals all suffering from diarrhea. And their vehicles were falling apart in the parking lot and shouldn't be allowed on the public roads. "One," he said, "nearly blew up in the parking lot, backfiring all over Janitor Jeff.

This guy is good, I thought. As one who occasionally strays from the truth, I appreciate someone's ability to tell a good story. I still didn't know if I had fooled him or not, but I doubt it. The incident was never mentioned again. He was a good principal.

Mr. Fitness

I might have been in the best shape of my life the week I started teaching school for the first time. I had started that summer spending 30 days at Camp Pendleton being a Marine. Then I spent almost 3 full months unloading boxcars, or cleaning warehouses after a flood. And doing it at a mile above sea level. Yucca Valley was approximately 60% of that altitude.
I was shocked and couldn't believe the poor shape some of my students were in. Many were overweight enough to be classified as obese. I decided one of my goals would be to have the most physically fit fifth grade in San Bernardino County. I told my class my idea of turning them into little supermen and superwomen. [5]

---

[5] 3,369 feet

They were for it. I told them I would join them in this little project and become the fittest 5th-grade teacher in the state of California. That got me a round of applause. The plan was for the first month for them to jog or power walk one lap around the entire field and then every day to add ten steps.

It was just after the two o'clock recess that I kept them out on the playground. I lined them up behind the tether balls and off we went with me in the lead. Several soon passed me, but I felt I could reel them in if I stayed close. I was concentrating on not being beat by those in front and not looking back at those behind. When I did, I saw some walking, some limping, some sitting, and some lying on the ground prostrate. *This cannot be good Wheatley*, I told myself. I imagine that's the way the field looked after the Battle of Bull Run or Gettysburg. I blew my whistle calling off the rest of the jog to the few that were still upright and moving. I went back to see if I was facing open revolt or murder charges.

Nobody was belligerent. They just said they couldn't finish. I promised them I would rethink the distances and the timetable. We limped back to the classroom. They were all at least 75% recovered by the time school got out.

But they looked like they had been ridden hard and put away wet.

The next morning; I received a summons to report to the principal's office. The principal and the school nurse were waiting for me and loaded for bear. They told me their phones had not stopped ringing all night.

Then they went on to explain that many families had moved up to the high desert to get away from the pollution below because their children had asthma and had trouble breathing.

It was suggested that I leave physical training up to people like Paul Bragg and Jack LaLane and concentrate on the 5th Grade curriculum.

Reeves

I wasn't the only male hire that year. Reeves was a graduate of Western New Mexico University. He was a good teacher, quite handsome, and SINGLE. That sort of made him the center of attention. He and I became good friends and even coached a Little League team together.

Professional Organizations

The first year I joined the National Education Association (NEA), The California Teachers Association (CTA), and the local Morongo Teacher's Association (MTA). It took quite a bite out of the Wheatley budget. The district was quite proud that it had 100% membership in all three associations.

At this time Ronald Reagan was running to be the Governor of California against Pat Brown. After listening to both men and their ideas, I decided Mr. Reagan was the better choice.

The CTA did not agree with me and was throwing its support (money) behind Brown. I decided to become an ex-member of the CTA. I still joined the NEA and MTA. That is not completely true. The local district (MTA) had a rule that unless you joined the other two, you couldn't join them. The NEA was not quite so picky.

I became the only teacher in the whole district that didn't join all three. The Morongo School District could no longer claim they were 100% in all three organizations. They were 99.8% in two and 100% in only one: the NEA.

They would probably have been happy to see me leave, but I was a good teacher when I wasn't trying to kill the kids with laps of the school. The kids liked me and were learning. Their parents liked me because their students did so well, and I had friends on the school board. At the end of my third year, I was offered tenure but didn't take it because we were going back to Colorado so Grace could get her degree before Auntie keelhauled me. But I'm getting ahead of myself. I'll tell you about that later.

House Hunting

All was not well in Camelot (house on the hill). The first problem was the scarcity of water and the cost to have the water tank behind the house filled. My bride did not support my water conservation project. She kept wanting to drink the stuff and take a shower every week.

But there also appeared to be some kind of electrical problem. We would get little shocks when touching the faucet in the kitchen.

One day when Grace was down in the valley shopping, I decided to surprise her by doing the dishes. I remember reaching for the faucet and not much after that.

Grace said when she returned that I was sitting in the middle of the kitchen on the floor and singing Hank William's song about "I Saw the Light."

"Have you been curling your hair?" she asked.

"No. Why?"

"It's curly. It wasn't curly when I left for town."

Back At the Ranch (Gallup)

Back in Gallup, Chick was getting anxious to get his station wagon back. The sarge and Big Donna had been looking for an excuse to come visit us, so they said they would drive my little car out and the station wagon back. That would be perfect I thought. I asked Sarge to bring his electrical tools with him because there was something wrong with the wiring. He was flattered, but he was not really that good of an electrician.

The day they arrived, I met them downtown. Grace stayed behind to put finishing touches on the house and the meal she had prepared.

Watching Sarge and Big Donna climb out of the little car was a painful sight. Neither one of them could stand up straight. They had been folded in the fetal position in the tiny car for eight hours . . . AND . . . seventeen minutes. I tried to straighten them out, but as soon as I'd let go that person would snap back into the folded position.

Finally I said after several unsuccessful tries, "Do you want to follow me to the house? Grace is waiting for us and she has prepared a fine dinner." I started heading for the station wagon.

"**HALT!**" commanded the Sarge. **"We, Donna and I, will take the station wagon and you may have the sardine can."**

After a delicious dinner, we visited outside as we watched the town turn from day to night. Grace and Big Donna visited about friends, relatives, clothes, and other lady things. I told Sarge about the electrical shocks, but the house wouldn't perform. It was on its best behavior. It was like going to the dentist and not being able to remember which tooth it was that was giving you concern.

"I'll check it out tomorrow," he said. I noticed he was still walking bent over and so was Big Donna.

The next day I took the ladies shopping and Sarge stayed behind and worked on the electricity. When we got back, he was sitting on the kitchen floor singing "I Saw the Light." I helped him to his feet and noticed he was standing straight.

The house went back into one of its good behavior spells. They left the next day thinking he had fixed our problem. The next day I saw the light again.

We started looking in earnest for a house we could safely afford to rent long-term. Things were a little better because I had already received two paychecks.

The house we found to rent was on an unpaved sandy road and had originally been a carport. But the plumbing and electricity didn't bite, and the price was right. We now had a permanent place. The house had a large fenced-in backyard for Petrarch, a bathroom, a kitchen/dining room (breakfast nook), a bedroom, and a living room. It was just the right size for that period in our lives.

But we were bothered by the fact that we might have lost the friendship of our guardian angels. We worried they would think we were not appreciative of all they and their friends had done for us. We were afraid they would hold it against us.

But angels don't do that or act like that. One day, I believe it was the first part of November they and some members of their church showed up at our new place bearing gifts.

They brought every possible thing someone expecting a baby could want. There were baby clothes, booties, blankets, towels, knitted hats, sweaters, socks, shampoo, baby oil, baby wash, baby lotion, nose cleaner, 12 baby bottles, 1 baby bottle brush, baby bathtub, bassinette, changing table, plastic changing sheets, chest of drawers that had a little closet on one side and 4 drawers on the other, 2 huge boxes of cloth diapers, 2 boxes of diaper pins, baby toys, rattles.

AND some BIG hugs.

It was a friendship that lasted a lifetime, long after we left the valley, mainly through books, cards, and letters. I still consider the time spent with Bob and Jane one of the greatest experiences of my life.

Neckties

I hate to wear ties. They make me feel like someone's hands are around my throat. I hate peoples' hands around my throat. I like neckties as much as I like chopped liver and only a little more than I like broccoli.

During my second year at Yucca Valley everything was going so well I was starting to get cocky. I came up with a plan to do away with the dreaded necktie. I would use the principle of gradualism. I tried to get Reeves to join me, but he wouldn't.

The first step was to get the principal to accept the bolo tie as being equal to the cloth tie. Fortunately, I had some beautiful bolo ties because the Sarge was in charge of about 30 Indian silversmiths. Indian jewelry was the presents I received on my birthdays and Christmas.

I was really nervous the first day of my campaign because Marvin ran a tight ship. The bolo tie I chose had a large piece of Bisbee Turquois inset into a silver frame with intricate designs. Nothing was said.

I had pulled it off. The next step was to lower the tie an inch. The week after that, I lowered it two inches. On the third week, it was lowered three inches. I no longer had the feeling of hands around my throat. I should have.

I should have left well enough alone or stopped there. The following Monday I left the tie at home. I left all my ties at home.

That afternoon after school I got the message to report to the principal's office. The secretary told me to go right in, that he was expecting me. She whispered, "By the way, good luck."

Principal Marvin was working with some papers on his desk or pretending to. He looked up, signaled me to wait and then went back to his papers. He did not give me permission to sit. I stood in front of his desk for five minutes waiting and imagining all kinds of dire thoughts. I was wishing with all my heart that my collar was buttoned and I was wearing a tie and looking professional. I pictured headlines in the local paper **"FIFTH GRADE TEACHER SHOT BY PRINCIPAL FOR DRESS CODE VIOLATIONS."**

After five minutes, it seemed like five days, the principal looked up at me. Then he pointed at his own throat. He was wearing a beautiful tie perfectly tied with a Windsor knot. Then he said, "That will be all," and he went back to whatever he was doing with those papers.

I got the message. I would be wearing a tie the next day. The dress code for teachers was a lot stricter back in the 1960s. Marvin was a good principal. He was able to maintain control without causing bad feelings.

Yucca Valley Snow

Jimmie Durante had a hit record many years ago called "I Remember the Day I Read a Book." Well I remember the day it snowed in Yucca Valley. I was there three years and it snowed once, but that was enough. It produced maybe twelve inches, but that was enough. Twelve inches in Yucca Valley was like three feet in Gallup, Fort Collins, or Durango.

It was beautiful when I got up and put the dog out. My Boxer, Petrarch, was beside himself. He had never seen snow before. He was jumping straight up and down and reminded me of a little boy on a pogo stick. I couldn't tell if he was jumping for joy or trying to keep his feet out of the cold stuff.

On my drive to work, I passed house after house where the owners had made snowmen, none of them very high. It made me feel like Swift's Gulliver in the lands of the little people. (Lilliput & Blefuscu)

I got to school and was told that school was cancelled. I phoned Grace and told her to stay put because it was dangerous out there. I was not kidding. On the way over and back, I witnessed cars sailing through intersections, several crashes, and ditches full of cars waiting for a wrecker to pull them out.

Yucca Valley did not have sand and gravel set aside for a snowy day. The town did not have snow plows. The closest were probably up at Big Bear (70 miles away) and they were probably wrestling with several feet or more of the white stuff from the same storm.

By evening the snow had mostly melted and everything was nearly back to normal except for those who were trying to reach their auto-insurance agent.

"The Desert Wind"

You have to take everything I say with a grain of salt . . . or is it sugar you are supposed to take it with? How about catsup or Tabasco? Mayonnaise? Mustard?

Remember how in my first book "Marry Merry Mary Christmas,"_on Page 219 (the page that tells about the author) I wrote, "in Yucca Valley, as an adult, Pete edited the popular Desert Wind." I was hoping to give the impression that I was an experienced editor and writer. AND NOW (if I may quote Paul Harvey) ". . . FOR THE REST OF THE STORY."

One day after school and the students had gone home, I was in my room correcting papers when the principal walked in. This was shortly after the necktie episode. Luckily I was still wearing mine. Most days I took it off when the last bus cleared the parking lot.

I started to stand. He signaled me to stay seated. That way I would have to look-up at him, placing him in the power position.

"I think the school needs a school newspaper," he said.

You're entitled to think anything you want, I thought. *But why are you telling me,* I asked myself. I did not like the possible answers I was coming up with. I didn't have any extra time in my day, and something called Modern Math was trying to eat my lunch. But I did not transfer what I was thinking to my face, a trick my dad had taught me when he was teaching my brother and I how to play poker. He also taught us not to gamble by winning our allowance for the month . . . and keeping it.

"I knew you'd be excited," the principal said.

"What gave it away? My yawn?"

He scowled. "I'm making you the editor and chief. Get Reeves to help you. By the way, nice tie." He turned and left.

The *Desert Wind* was popular though not always favorably. It depended on whose ox was getting gored. (Another favorite quote of my dad's.) My ox was gored when one of the reporters pointed out I was "down right mean. Another pointed out that I had two moles on my face and wore a watch that was hardly ever correct.

The Wind was several pages pumped out on a mimeograph machine after school once a month. Somehow copies of it ended up being read and discussed over many dinner tables, at PTA meetings, Kenny's Barber Shop and other interesting locations.

My mother saved some of the copies. I'll see if I can find them and share some of the gems with you.

I was working on the first edition of the school newspaper and listening to the radio when the song "The Summer Wind" came on. It gave me the idea for the name of the paper. I would change it from the exciting YUCCA VALLEY ELEMENTARY SCHOOL NEWSPAPER to THE DESERT WIND.

I can't remember who was singing. It was either Wayne Newton or Frank Sinatra. I tried to write my own words to the melody. I would get Grace to record it on our tape recorder and play it in each classroom to promote the paper.

This is what I came up with:
The Desert Wind came scorching in
Across my knees
It burned my face, a middle place,
And then my feet
All summer long
It played ping pong
With Rocks & Sand & Trees
My persistent friend
The Desert Wind
The little tykes
Came in Buses on Bikes
For us to teach
To fill a need, learn to read
And do what's right
We were strong 'n young, it was a job well done,
'Mongst the Yuccas and Joshua Trees
And the Desert Wind seemed like the Desert Breeze

I wrote more verses, some equally bad and some worse. I decided to forget song writing. If I didn't like it, I knew no one else would.   Each month each class would turn into me what they were doing. (I will not bore you with these.) Then there was a sports section, a personality of the month (usually a teacher), awards (usually a student), and whatever tickled my fancy. Any gaps, I filled in with jokes or my unique observations. That is where I first heard the expression that has haunted me ever since: "Nobody will think it's funny."

...   The drawing of the staff was left on my desk as I was preparing the last issue for the school year. We came back to the classroom after recess and it was on my desk. I liked it. I liked it so much that I decided to put it in the paper. I had no idea who drew it, but there were some clues. I'll share the clues with you, and maybe together we can figure it out.

Clue #1: Nobody from Kindergarten, First or Second Grade was in it, so I eliminated those folks.

Clue #2: The picture of the custodians should have reminded me of two geometric shapes: the circle and the rectangle, not two rectangles. I will call them Mutt and Jeff after the comic strip characters of the same shape. Mutt and Jeff had access to every room in the school. And because we were used to seeing them all over the school, nobody would think it strange to see them coming out of my room, especially if they were carrying brooms. Also, one of them could act as a look-out for the other. I filed them in my mind as "persons of interest."

Clue #3: Then there was the principal. He was a short man in the real world, yet in the picture he was the tallest. The picture showed both him and me prominently wearing neckties. I thought only he and I knew about the necktie incident.

The part of my life, the one I call "Pete the Private Detective," closed as quickly as it opened. It's right up there with "Song Writing Pete." This mystery has remained unsolved and has been placed in my "Cold Cases" file.

But I have a feeling that it was the school secretary. She knew everything that happened in that school, and in the picture, her character is placed higher than all the rest of us and has angel wings. However, no one reported seeing her out of the office or in the vicinity of my classroom that day, and I find it unbelievable that SHE would leave out the K. thru 2nd grade teachers. Despite that, I still believe it was either Mrs. Hutchinson or Cornel Mustard in the cafeteria with a magic marker.

I really don't remember the lower grade teachers, but starting with the third grades and running through the fifth, there were two of each: 3rd grade, Duval & Youngberg; 4th grade, Jessup & Reeves; 5th grade, Lofgren & Wheatley.

Duval was the lively bride of a Marine and would often challenge students to jump roping contests when on yard duty. Youngberg was short and cute. One student wrote in the paper that she was the most attractive of all the teachers. I never liked her or that particular student after that.

Jessup was a good teacher and saved our bacon several times with her musical ability, like at the Christmas programs. Reeves was a good teacher and a good friend. Reeves had a television. Grace and I didn't. He loved lording it over me and loved telling me what I had missed. His particular favorite show was Batman.

Mrs. Lofgren was wonderful. She was solid, a great teacher, and had grown up on a farm. She had many years teaching experience and shared her knowledge with me as I was making every mistake a first year teacher could make.

There were so many things that popped up daily that they didn't teach us about in college, like the first time a student threw up in the classroom and the custodians were hiding. Her advice was, "Quit your crying, suck it up, and clean it up, Butter Cup."

There was a school nurse who even contributed several articles on dental health to the paper. She broke her leg skiing. One of the students wrote her up as a personality of the month. There was Mrs. Stiles the Special Ed. Teacher. I used to make fun of her because she only had eight students where the rest of us averaged thirty-five. She challenged me to switch classes with her for a day. I lasted one hour. If I had tried for a second hour, the men in the white coats might have been coming for me. After that hour, I was her biggest fan and supporter.

Mr. Lopez was the music teacher. He was young, with a pregnant wife, played the violin and was loved by all. He came during my third year.

Principal Marvin was the boss, and you might notice that he is depicted in the picture as being the biggest, even though he was not the tallest. I thought he was a good principal but just a little too preoccupied and gave too much importance to things like bulletin boards, penmanship, neckties, and clean green grass.

On the upper right of the picture is Mrs. Hutchinson. Like I've already said, I believe she is the one that really ran the school. She might often have to trick Marvin into doing what she wanted, just the way my mom used trickery to get what she wanted at home. In most of the schools I worked at, it was really the secretary that ran the school and the one you went to if you wanted things done. Mrs. Hutchison was the best at it.

I have made a model of the paper taking parts from several different issues. It was not an easy job. The ink has faded to being almost invisible in the last 50 years.

DESERT WIND

Lovely Teeth

Are the Heart of a Smile

In cooperation with the American Dental Association we are announcing the 18th National Dental Health Education February 1966.

You students are learning the value of

BLAH BLAH BLAH..............

Dee Dee Church

School Nurse

Sports

Soccer

Lonnie Jones

The school championship of Yucca Valley Elementary School was decided this month. Mr. Reeve's class after a rather disappointing season came on to win the championship.

New Games

Ricky Smith

The principle has come up with some games that will help us develop our muscles while keeping us safe.

Weather Report

The storm warnings are up for all students who did not do well this quarter. Grades are coming out on Thursday.

Despite prayers and rain dances the Yucca Valley school went for a whole quarter without a day off because of bad weather.

. . .

Why is no one afraid of the dogwood tree. It's bark is worse than its bite.

BOY OH BOY

Getting revenge for all the innocent students who have suffered under the tyrant Mr. Wheatley, the stork picked out the meanest, noisiest baby he had and delivered it to the teacher.

The baby weighed in at six pounds and fourteen ounces and his height was nineteen inches. His name is Thomas Lyle Wheatley.

It would be appreciated if the students would be nice to Mr. Wheatley because he is not getting as much sleep as he used to.

Construction Begins

Work on the new classrooms began with the leveling of the land by a "Cat" and a "Euc."

It would be appreciated if the students would not lean on the restraining fence while watching and directing the work and workers.

Safety Council Report

Dean Jordan

In the December issue your safety committee reported that a committee had been formed to speak to the principal concerning the return of jump ropes to the playground. It is my pleasure to report that the request has been granted.

The Safety Committee wishes to thank Principal W. for his approval and at the same time speak to you to please help us keep this privilege for your pleasure by using the jump ropes for jumping only and not as a weapon of destruction or to tie up other kids.

Guess Who

The object of this game is to try and guess who the students are trying to describe. I have separated some of the guessers with three dots.

He is slightly fat...He eats a lot, but it doesn't look like it...This person is chubby...He is very calm when people get mad at him...He is a little plump and tells Mr. Wheatley what happened on Batman...He doesn't give much homework and he won't let my sister bring Kool aide to school. GUESS WHO

He is nice. He teaches well. He is nice. His wife is going to have a baby. He has black hair and dark skin. GUESS WHO.

My brother says she gets mad awfully easy...She is short and wears sunglasses...She smiles a lot and is the prettiest of the teachers. GUESS WHO

She wears a whistle around her neck...She often tells me to be quiet...She gets mad at me for no reason when I am bad. GUESS WHO

This person is rather heavy and round and has hardly any hair...He looks like Santa Claus without a beard. He has blue eyes and wears gray clothes...He carries a broom all over the school...He cleans and fixes thing...He tells everyone to get out of the bathroom...He is jolly and winks at just about everyone he sees. GUESS WHO

She has curly, dark black hair. She wears glasses. She is very trim and her skin is darker than most people. GUESS WHO

She has red hair, wears glasses and is very nice. She helps Mr. W in the office in many ways and runs errands. GUESS WHO

He is young and friendly...He is downright mean...This person sits on his desk, wears glasses, has blue eyes, and is very strong...He has a watch that is hardly any good...He has two moles on his face and doesn't yell too often (Grr Ed.)...He wears glasses and keeps the container for them hooked to his belt. GUESS WHO

All she thinks about are teeth and shots. She takes very good care of her teeth, but not her legs. She smiles and limps a lot. GUESS WHO

She has musical talent. She has short reddish hair that is actually a flip. She is about 5' 4". She is very nice. GUESS WHO.

This person is often seen jumping rope with us. It doesn't take much to get her mad. She has black hair and is the tallest woman teacher. She is from Tennessee. GUESS WHO.

This person has brown eyes, wears glasses, and is about 6' tall. Kids visit him often. He is the boss of the teachers. Most of the time he is very strict. He has a little bald spot on top of his head. He likes to sit in the office with his feet on the desk. GUESS WHO

Glasses

We were on the freeway heading up to visit my Aunt Betty and her family in La Crescenta where I had grown up. There had been many changes on the freeway system since I had left California for Alaska, so I was pretty much dependent on the Big Signs telling me where to exit & enter. In that same time period, someone had found a way to make the signs fuzzier and hard to read from a distance. By the time I could read "Pasadena Freeway" it was too late.

It took me a while to get back to the exit I had missed. Disrespect and road rage was running rampant. (Say that ten times as fast as you can. When I try, the last word becomes "rabbit.")

"You need to get your eyes checked," said my wife.

"If you're not going to move it, build a porch on it, shouted a passing motorist whose car and owner both needed an improved muffler. I don't think he had ever seen someone driving the speed limit before.

"You know," I said to Grace. "I think one of us needs to get their eyes checked."

"Duh," said Grace. "Either that or get **HIM** a white cane." She had been on my case ever since the incident in the school library at Fort Lewis.

The Incident: I had walked into the library where I was to join Grace. I spotted her and went over to her table and sat down. I was truly not in the mood to study, so I suggested, "Let's get out of here and do something fun." (I winked at her) Then I reached across the table and gently closed the book she had been reading and reached for her hand.

"It sounds nice, and I am flattered," she said, "but I have a test tomorrow and I need to study." She pulled her hand free and reopened the book.

"It hit me like a ton of books, uh bricks, uh ton of anything. I jumped up and declared, "**YOU** . . . ARE NOT GRACE!"

"I'm aware of that," she said calmly.

"You're not Grace," I repeated in disbelief.

"I know. I'm Peggy."

Students and librarians were making sounds like a punctured tires. "SHUSH." And saying things like "Knock it off." A girl that had been working a few tables away got up and came over. I thought it was a librarian.

"She's not Grace," I told the librarian, pointing at the sitting girl.

"I know, I am Grace." Grace had watched me enter the library and walk over to the table with the pretty girl and start flirting. She had sat there getting madder and madder until she heard her name mentioned, and then she came over. The real librarian was the next to join this noisy little pow wow. She pointed at me and said, "I think you had better leave."

I tried to explain, but she kept pointing towards the exit and repeating the word "OUT" and something about "… or I'll call campus security." Until then, I had been thinking of telling her that I was a tax payer and that she worked for me, but when she mentioned campus security, I decided to take the higher moral ground. I picked up my books and exited. Grace and her opinions followed me out.

That was the first time Grace mentioned that I might have needed to get my eyes checked. I blamed the incident on the fluorescent lighting in the library and the fact I had been up all night finishing a book report on Moby Dick for an American Literature class. That's a big book. The next day my sight was back to normal.

Back to the present. I would have put off getting my eyes checked, but I was about due to get my Driver's License renewed and they often make you read an eye chart.

I did not realize how much my eyesight had changed until I got my glasses. Suddenly the trees had individual leaves. Green grass was made up of blades of grass. I could recognize people from a distance and read signs on the freeway in plenty of time. I didn't have to squint, and the list goes on.

Without realizing it, I had been living in a make-believe world. In it, everything was like in a painting. Now I could see everything in crystal clear reality. But having my sight restored was not all good. Now I could see warts and moles on people's faces, litter in the streets, and smog to name a few. When I caught my reflection in a mirror or store window, I no longer saw Superman. I saw Clark Kent.

Walking in the rain was no longer fun, as the drops clung to my glasses inhibiting my vision. However, the benefits outweighed the disadvantages, and I wore glasses for the next 30 years.

It seemed like at each annual checkup, I needed a stronger prescription and when I wasn't wearing them that everything beyond the end of my nose was out of focus. And *eye* (a little play on words) have a very short nose.

Baseball

Reeves claimed he had coached a champion Little League team in Albuquerque. So he became the manager of the Yucca Valley Dodgers, and I was his assistant. We were told we'd be lucky to win one game. The good old boys already knew who the stars would be and had divided them up between themselves. All we were left with were the unknowns. During a practice game we lost 18 to 2. We got to bat first. The game ended in the first inning. We managed to get two outs on the other guys before the game was called because it was too dark to continue.

About that time according to the Desert Wind, Principal Marvin came up with a game called Puntball. The idea was to score a touchdown you had to punt it across the other guy's goal line. Principal Marvin was trying to prevent injuries.

To add to my troubles, a tall kid I will call Charlie transferred in and was placed in my class. I tried everything I knew to get him put in Lofgren's class, but she had one more student than I did and she was too wise and tricky to allow me to succeed. Charlie had problems with math and reading.

We were out in the playground and I was introducing the class to Marvin's Puntball. I had the class divided in half. Dean and Ricky were the captains and had chosen the players on their teams. It came out uneven so I filled in on Ricky's team. The game was pretty even with Dean's team getting a little the better of it. We were about to get scored on when I caught the ball on the run and gave it a mighty kick. It drove the other team all the way back almost to their five yard line.

Nice kick Mr. Wheatley," I heard several say. I was proud, but it didn't last. The ball came flying back. It flew over all our heads and scored for the other guys. *What in the world.* The kid Charley had kicked the ball farther than my best kick ever. Nearly every time Charlie kicked the ball it was a score. I was beginning to hate Puntball.

As we were going back to class an idea occurred to me. I said, "Go long Charlie," and threw the football with everything I had. It was a decent effort and should have gone over his head, but he caught up with it easily and plucked it out of the air.

"Go long, Mr. Wheatley," he shouted. I took off with every ounce of speed I could muster. I looked up and saw it sailing over my head.

"Sorry, Mr. Wheatley," he shouted.

"Charlie, . . . "

"Yes Sir."

"What do you think of baseball?"

"My favorite sport."

Reeves and I gave Charlie a secret tryout. He could out throw both of us. Neither one of us could strike him out, and most of his hits would have been homeruns in a game. We asked if he had ever pitched. "That was my position last year," he said. He struck Reeves out three times and me out 16 times. The kid was a pheromone. We checked his records in the office. He was the right age to play. Now we had to keep him a secret until the rosters were set and official.

For the rest of the week, physical education class in my room consisted of musical chairs, Simon says, hide and seek, red light/green light, and the quiet game. Reeves did not want the news of Charley's ability to get out.

I forgot to tell Charley about the try outs. But I went to the other teams and told them I had a boy in my 5th grade class who had missed a lot of school this year because of ill health, and I'd like to put him on the team hoping that would help him take an interest in school. They were all feeling over confident thinking they had really pulled the wool over our eyes. We were the new kids on the block. The Pirates had been the champs for the last three years. They all figured one 5th grader added to the Dodgers wouldn't make that much difference even if he was good.

I was not like those other sneaky coaches and managers. I felt honor bound to warn them. I didn't want anything on my conscience. I warned them he was a fine athlete and mentioned he was the champion hide-and-seeker and quiet game player in my class.

Our first game was against a team that usually finished the season in second or third place. We won 4 to 0. Charley pitched a no-hitter and hit three homeruns. You should have heard the squawking. A fox in the henhouse couldn't have caused more commotion. Charley went through a stiffer vetting than the president of the United States. He was legal.

Teams quit pitching to him. They walked him. One time they let the ball get too close to the plate and he smacked it for a triple. Even when they walked him he was dangerous. He was so fast he would steal his way around to third, then take advantage of any opportunity to score. They countered this by walking the batter in front of Charley to clog up the base paths so he couldn't steal. The Dodgers won the League that year. Charley and Reeves got most of the credit.

Disneyland

On Grace's Birthday, I surprised her by taking her to Disneyland. She dressed up and looked real pretty. She was wearing a blue blouse and the beautiful skirt made out of Hilpert's pants.

She knew it was her birthday, but that is all she knew. I just told her it was a surprise.

As we headed down from Yucca Valley her first guess was Desert Hot Springs (swimming) or Palm Springs (movie, fancy restaurant, and tram to the top of the mountain). I had put a suitcase in the trunk to throw her off track. It would make her think we were staying overnight. But I turned west in the other direction and she figured we were going to visit relatives. When I turned away from the way to the relatives, she didn't know where we were going. She didn't know until we pulled into the Disneyland parking lot.

She had never been there before and had always wanted to go. She was so excited and enjoyed everything, even the tram ride in from a distant parking lot. The train near the entrance (Casey Jr.) that circled the park was our first ride followed by Small World. She was like the biggest happiest child in the park.

They wouldn't let her on some of the scarier rides because of her pregnancy, but she was able to do most. As the sun got low on the horizon, I told her we only had time for one more. She said she really wanted to do the Teacups but was afraid they wouldn't let her. When we got near the front of the line, she came up with a plan to fool them.

She put on the coat she had been carrying and took a large bag I had been carrying and held it before her tummy. On a day when everyone was dressed like for a tennis match, she hit the front of the line looking like someone going on an arctic expedition, holding a bag at extended port arms in front of her tummy to cover the bulge. Her arms were straight out.

The man checking tickets let us pass with a smile on his face. "Guess I fooled him," she said with a smile as we settled down in our teacup. I don't think the park thought of the Teacup ride as being frightening.

She never stopped chattering all the way home. She said it was the best birthday she had ever had. Come to think of it, I can't remember one I enjoyed more either. Well . . . maybe this was my second favorite. My first bicycle had slipped into third place.

The Big Bear Went Over the Mountain

I have good judgment. They say people with good judgment got that way by having bad judgment. They could be right. One day I took Grace and Petrarch the dog for a ride to Big Bear Lake a distance of 70 miles. We had a lovely time up there in the pines. It was almost like being in Colorado except there were more people.

On the way back we were tired and anxious to get home after playing hard. I passed a sign that said Pioneer Town 25 miles and it had an arrow pointing off to the right. I knew Pioneer Town was 10 miles from Yucca Valley. Thirty-five miles sounded a lot better than seventy miles, so I turned right. That was my first step in improving my judgment. The road turned from pavement to dirt.

"What are you doing?"

"Saving us thirty-five miles."

It was suddenly like riding a rollercoaster. After that it became like rafting on a river: periods of calm between periods of rapids. It took all my skill to keep us upright. I wasn't sure if I was tearing up things under the car or not.

This could have proved to be the most expensive thirty-five miles I had ever saved. I have never been too lucky with shortcuts. We came to a flat area, and I stopped to see how much damage had been done to the car. Grace and the dog joined me.

"Not too many Sunday drivers out today," she commented. (We had not seen anyone since we started down the shortcut, not even a mountain goat. "I wonder why no one else is interested in saving 35 miles," she opined.

I was not in the mood for idle conversation, so I kept quiet.

This was in the days before cell phones which is the only thing that kept me from phoning Triple A or Bob Purcell.

"How are you at delivering babies?" Grace asked.

"**ALL ABOARD**," I shouted in my best train conductor voice. Actually, it was in my best train conductor's voice who has just learned that there is runaway train bearing down on him, and he needs to get his train safely on a siding out of the way.

Grace was no trouble, but the dog wanted no part of any more rides. He had been flipped all over the car during our first decent. I decided to let him follow the car for a while.

I told Grace we could put an ad in the paper if he didn't rejoin us. "Lost Dog last seen somewhere between Big Bear and Pioneer Town. Purebred Boxer. NO REWARD."

Everything went well until we rounded a corner and found ourselves facing a humongous boulder in the middle of the trail, about the size of a small house. On one side of the boulder was mountain. On the other side, space. By space, I mean a drop-off.

"Well, up jumped the Devil," said Grace. (It was a favorite expression of her father when things were not going well.) We got out and started trying to figure out what to do. The dog caught up with us and jumped in the car without being asked. We had dropped enough altitude that desert conditions prevailed. Petrarch must have decided if he was going to die, it would be by rolling down the side of a mountain in a car rather than of heat stroke.

Using my hands to measure, I thought I could get by the boulder with a full 3 inches (4 fingers) to spare. A larger car wouldn't have a chance. I was pretty sure the car would not be able to make the climb back to Big Bear.

"Mind if I watch from out here?" Grace asked.

"I insist on it." I couldn't get the dog out of the car. I looked at Grace and saluted, "We who are about to die salute you," I quoted. Petrarch barked something in Boxer. Grace said something about she hoped her next husband registered a little higher on the IQ charts. We crept by the boulder at a snail's pace, an inch at a time.

We made it and didn't even scrape any paint off the car. I asked my very pregnant wife if she thought **she** could get by the boulder. She threw a rock at me. Some people have no appreciation for my wonderful sense of humor.

Fortunately, the shortcut only added about an hour to the trip and did no noticeable damage to the car.

That was the week before the baby was born.

Baby Runs

I never drove faster, before or since. I had seen movies where taxi drivers, cops, and boyfriends were forced by necessity to deliver babies because the baby didn't want to wait. I did not want to be in that position.

Months in advance of the baby's birth I knew to the millisecond the fastest route to the hospital from any location in Yucca Valley. No run would take longer than fourteen minutes and thirty-six seconds.

I had driven every possible way as fast as I could from all likely locations with Grace in the passenger seat holding a stopwatch, pen, paper, and clipboard. She thought I was driving dangerously, especially when I would cut through someone's yard, cross a vacant lot, race up an alley, or run a stop sign if there were no other cars around. I believe it is called a California Rolling Stop. And we were in California. I let her scream during these practice runs figuring it just added to the reality.

Baby Birth Day

Towards the start of the holidays, Grace's doctor put her on a schedule of once-a-week doctor visits. I figured this meant, "<u>anytime</u>" I was about to be a papa. Anytime I wasn't teaching school, I was following her around with the keys to the car on a shoelace necklace around my neck, and I was carrying a catcher's mitt just in case there wasn't time to make it to the hospital. (Just joking about the catcher's mitt.)

I lost five pounds and countless hours of sleep during that first week. One week of a baby being overdue is equal to five normal weeks. The first week, nothing happened followed by: Nothing happened, followed by Nothing happened. Followed by Nothing happened.

Thanksgiving came and went. I had turned down an invitation to join the Smiths for that holiday because I didn't want to be over fourteen minutes and thirty-six seconds away from the Yucca Valley Hospital and Doctor A.

At first, when I took her for a weekly checkup I was sure that would be the day, but after so many visits I was less sure than the week before. I even read up and became an expert on false pregnancies. I broached the subject with the doctor. He assured me, "Grant, I promise, Scouts Honor, there is a baby in there. It's just not its time. "

I thought Grace was expanding at an alarming rate. I was afraid she might explode. In fact, she did. I suggested one night while we were lying in bed that she face in the other directions just in case. She exploded but it was verbally. I would have changed doctors, but his daughter was in my class and my best student. I was counting on her for the big spelling bee.

My Uncle Jim, a vice president of Pauley Petroleum, had been attending a convention in Palm Springs. He was my mother's oldest brother. He and his wife Virginia decided to drive up to Yucca Valley and see how we were doing. They stopped by our house and had a nice visit with Grace and then she said, "I have to go for my weekly checkup with my doctor."

They offered to take her, not wanting the visit to end. When it was her turn to see the doctor, they said they would drive over to the school and pick me up. Then take us out to dinner.

Grace was feeling so good, no one had any idea that the grand event would be that night. She had even considered skipping this doctor visit in honor of Jim and Virginia popping in. To be completely honest with you, we were hoping ours would be the first baby born in '66. There were a lot of goodies that went along with that honor. In many respects, our cupboards were like that of Old Mother Hubbard.

After the examination, the doctor told Grace it is time to induce labor. "WHOA NELLIE," she said. "I've still got three more weeks. My husband figured it out mathematically, and he is a whiz bang at math. Besides, we have unexpected company, and tonight would just not be convenient."

He must have seen something because he shook his head. "Do you have a ride to the hospital?"

"My husband will be here exactly at 4:30 p.m. We call him Punctual Pete. Say, what is that needle for? OUCH."

"It's called Pitocin and it will help your body do its part."

Next came the draining of the amniotic sac surrounding the fetus. (I looked up that name on the internet just to impress you. Did it work? It is a word I wouldn't normally use in three lifetimes.)

At exactly 4:30 she went out to wait for me. She was actually expecting me to already be there. I wasn't. Five minutes passed, ten minutes, fifteen minutes. She went back into the doctor's office and phoned the school. The secretary told her I had left with some relatives forty minutes ago. (There were no cell phones in those days.)

An hour went by with Grace waiting in the reception room. "Mrs. Wheatley, we are closing now," said the receptionist. "May I call you a taxi?"

Just at that moment, I burst in through the door. I was happy and joking. I had had the most delightful visit with Jim and Virginia. They were the type of people who were interested in everything. I had given them a tour of the school then some of the highlights of the town. And now they were going to take us out to dinner.

Grace mumbled something about water breaking as we walked to the car. I told her that was silly, you can't break water.

"Where would you like to go?" Uncle Jim asked as Grace climbed into their car.

"Hospital."

"Not necessary, "I said. "I showed them the hospital already."

"And five different ways to get there in under twelve and a half minutes," volunteered Aunt Virginia.

"Hospital," said Grace.

"What are you trying to tell us, Grace," asked Uncle Jim.

"Baby comes tonight. Maybe hospital. Maybe your car."

HOSPITAL" shouted Uncle Jim tromping on the gas.

"HOSPITAL," echoed Aunt Virginia even louder. (It was her car. Uncle Jim usually drove a company car.

"HOSPITAL," shouted Petrified Pete.

It was dark by now. All my practice runs had been done during the daylight hours. Everything looked different at night. We even got lost once and ended up on a dead-end road. That is when we turned around and headed for the lights of town and started over. We took all the main roads and obeyed all the traffic signs. The total trip took 32 minutes.

I checked Grace in, actually, I didn't. I just stood there looking stupid while she checked herself in. I realized the suitcase that had been packed for months waiting for this moment was back at our house next to the front door.

I would get Jim and Virginia to take me home and I would return in our car as fast as I could.

When we got to the house they said, "Good-Bye and Good Luck." That would have been all right if they had stopped there. But once started they found it hard to stop. They felt the need to critique my performance and their conclusion was that my performance had been less than stellar.

I hurriedly made a peanut butter sandwich, grabbed the suitcase that had been packed months in advance to be ready in case of emergency, and flew out the door. What do you think I forgot? I forgot my glasses. They were still in the kitchen next to an open jar of peanut butter. I had also forgot to put the lid back on. In all fairness, for the sake of accuracy, I must admit that I was not functioning at maximum efficiency.

The trip back took longer because things looked different at night and for some reason blurrier. The funny thing is I didn't realize I wasn't wearing glasses until I got back to the hospital. "Where are your glasses?" Grace asked when I walked into her room carrying the suitcase.

I was trying to decide if I had enough time to go for my glasses when the first set of contractions hit. BOY HOWDY, that was an experience. I believe my current hearing loss can be traced back to that moment
. The volume of sound coming out of that woman's mouth made me wonder if the hospital would sell me earplugs and probably shattered windows throughout the hospital.

She did get everyone's attention. There was no need for her to push any call buttons to alert the nurse's station. Grace was whizzed out of the room. I sat there dumbfounded and deaf. I had no idea what to do next. In the movies, the expectant father paces the floor in a waiting room smoking cigarettes. I wasn't a smoker. I wished I was.

A nurse came in and asked me something. I saw her mouth going up and down, but I was having trouble hearing her. I asked her to speak up or write it down. She wrote (1) DON'T SHOUT. (2) Would you like to watch?

I nodded. I asked the nurse if I could bum a cigarette from her. She just frowned. I asked if they couldn't give Grace something to calm her down. I don't know where they took her, but I could still hear her. She was the only thing I could hear. I asked if there was something the doctor could do to calm her down. By this time I was reading lips. The nurse said, yes, and he had already done it. He had given her a saddle blanket.

Well Whoopee Ti Yi Yo, I thought. *She's having a baby not going on a trail ride or cattle drive. What is it with these people?*

I learned later I had misread the nurse's lips. She had said "saddle block" not "saddle blanket." The nurse wrote "saddle block" on a sheet of paper and showed it to me. I had absolutely no idea what that was. But I nodded and smiled like I did.

The nurse led me down to a room and handed me some scrubs to put on. Next, I was taken to a washbasin where I scrubbed my hands and put on gloves. I was getting worried. Were they expecting me to participate?

Once I was bibbed and tuckered I was led to this large room with a big window. The window looked into the operating room.

In the middle of the room was a table and on the table was my wife, at least it sounded like Grace would sound if she were being mauled by a family of Grizzly Bears. Around the table was a group of masked individuals with their fingers in their ears. Between outbursts, they were doing something to the woman. But it was all too fuzzy for me to tell what, so I looked around the room on the other side of the window and the only thing that was halfway in focus for me was a medical cabinet with glass doors. And miracle of all miracles, in the glass doors I could see the reflection of what was happening in the middle of the room.

I saw the birth of my son in the reflection on a medical cabinet. It was like watching early television with poor reception. I think I must have unnerved several nurses and one doctor because they kept looking at me staring into the cabinet as much as they watched Grace. I have no idea what they were thinking, maybe that I was getting the lay of the land for a possible burglary.

When the operation was over, one of the masked people brought the baby over to the window and held him up for me to see. I had never seen anything . . . so . . . ugly in my life. It was red, wrinkled, and crying, yet . . . I felt an overpowering love for that . . .that . . . thing, matched only by the love I felt for my wife who was also looking red and wrinkled.

I don't remember much more about that night other than I stayed in Grace's room waiting for her to be returned to it. When she was, we didn't say much, just held hands. I held my tongue and didn't tell her or blame her, but I was thinking, "what in the world have you been eating to produce such an ugly . . .

She interrupted my thinking, "Have you seen the baby yet?" I nodded. "What do you think?" (Wrong question.)

"I think . . . that . . . it . . . is. . . the best-looking baby I have ever seen." I got away with it. The skies did not open and I did not get struck by lightning.

Finally, she said, "Phone Mama and Daddy and tell them they are grandparents. Then go to bed, you have school tomorrow."

When I got back to the house, I debated whether to call. Believe it or not, there were some people who didn't appreciate my phone calls after midnight or my wonderful sense of humor.

The phone rang 47 times before it was picked up by the sarge. He did not appear to be in a happy mood. "Do you know what time it is?"

"Is this the lady of the house?" I asked.

'HELL NO!" CLICK!

Well Self," I said to myself, "I tried." I climbed into bed, but I couldn't go to sleep. I was feeling guilty. I got out of bed and headed for the phone. This time it only rang 37 times before it was answered and not by the Sarge.

"Guess who this is."

"Telemarketer."

"No, it's your favorite son-in-law."

"Don't have one." (Up to this point, it was a repeat of an earlier phone call. We had worked out this telephone routine starting on the day after Grace and I got married.)

"Maybe this will help you remember. Last night through the considerable effort of your favorite son-in-law, you became a grandma. I'm surprised you were able to sleep through the event. No one in Yucca Valley was able to and I have heard that the San Andreas fault is showing unexpected activity."

I heard her yell at Sarge. "Gracie had a baby last night."

"Boy or Girl" I heard him ask. I think Donna wanted a girl to do girly things with and Sarge wanted a boy he could take hunting and fishing. I had been a complete disappointment in that area having grown up in the cities of southern California.

"It's a boy," I said. "Thomas Lyle Wheatley." (I named him after my last two roommates who had become good friends.)

Big Donna relayed the message. I heard Sarge in the background. "A boy, OH BOY."

Then she said something that took all the joy out of the moment. "I'm going to start packing and I will be out there later today or early tomorrow. I've got some people to talk to first and things to do."

"No . . . whoa . . . cease . . . stay." I was talking to myself she had hung up. She came and stayed between two or three weeks, and I am so glad she did. I'm not sure we could have handled it without her help.

After Birth

In those days there were none of the Sissy things like Pampers and Loves. In those days it was cloth diapers and the process of changing and cleaning was enough to make a grown man cry . . . and cough . . . and gag. (I witnessed this several times: first hand.)

I went through the gas chamber in the Marines and had to sing the Marine Corps Hymn three times before they'd let me out or put on my mask. That was a breeze compared to changing young Tom after a BM.

I don't know what they put in the baby's formula, but it could stop a charging rhino or a polar bear.

It wasn't that bad when she was breastfeeding, but that lasted about two days. I think Tom must have had coarse sandpaper gums.

Whenever I was taking care of the baby and Grace was scheduled to return within 30 minutes, I thought it a good time to teach him the benefits of delayed gratification.

Other times I would set him on the living room floor on a blanket, open the front door wide, go out on the porch and hyperventilate like I would when free diving; then I would run into the house and work until I was about to pass out. If I didn't pass out, I would run outside and repeat the cycle (breathe-work-run for air, breathe-work-run for air, breathe-work-run for air). It usually took three cycles for the kid and four for the diaper cleaning in the toilet. (That summer when I went looking for abalone with Uncle Jim off the coast of Catalina, he was impressed with how long I could stay down without any equipment. I just pretended I was changing one of Tommy's poopy diapers.

.   Diaper services were flourishing, but we didn't think we could afford them.

Everyone used glass baby bottles which needed to be sterilized. Grace would put them in boiling water then take them out and set them upside down on a plastic table cloth to dry. One day Petrarch grabbed the table cloth and gave it a jerk. Coincidentally that was the same day he became an outside dog.

Another exciting adventure was the baby's first bath. Grace was worried about having the house warm enough, so in addition to turning the heat all the way up, she set the oven to 400 degrees and left the oven door open. Before the first bath was over both she and the baby were sweating profusely. Adjustments were made for the next bath.

.

Little Fish

Reeves told me how he had gone swimming at Desert Hot springs over the weekend and all his aches and pains were gone. I didn't have any aches or pains, but I loved to swim. I was afraid I couldn't afford it because that's where the rich people came to get rid of aches.

Reeves said not a problem. He found a place off the main street that had been there for years and although not up to the standards of the snotty rich, was pretty good and affordable. He said the pool was good and the water just as healing. We decided to give it a try.

After playing around in the shallow end with the family, I decided to swim some laps. With each lap, I became more and more relaxed until I felt like I could hardly move.

It was an effort to drag myself out of the water and change into my street clothes. Grace had to drive us home. I was still feeling relaxed the next day, but I was able to move normally and had no sore muscles.

I tried the next weekend but paced myself. The results were great. It wasn't long until I was swimming in the hot springs pool once a week.

One day, I saw an article where someone was teaching babies how to swim. I applied the techniques to Tom and he was swimming before his first birthday.

I think we were the only ones under 70 that used that particular pool for swimming. The others mostly floated or walked around in the shallow end. Little Tom and his young parents were very popular.

Tom impressed his grandparents when we would meet them in Phoenix and he would swim in the heated pool at the Desert Hills motel with his grandpa.

Then we moved to Colorado and New Mexico where the water was cold and Tom lost his interest in swimming. By the time he was five, he had forgotten how to swim.

Tommy Terrific

Tom had the same advantage that I did. He was the first- born grandchild in the immediate family, as I was. Therefore, he was instant celebrity the instant he was born. We wore out four cameras taking pictures of him. Not only was he the first-born of his generation in the family, he was athletic, happy, smiling, photogenic, and had hair.

There are pictures of him doing pullups, swimming, flying through the air, and posing on top of the Jungle-Jim with his dad. We were young and dumb and thought we were invincible.

First Christmas

We decided to stay in southern California rather than to favor one set of parents over the other. At the last minute we decided to accept Uncle Wayne and Aunt Betty's invitation to spend Christmas with them and drove up to La Crescenta.

This Aunt Betty was Mom's younger sister. Way back when I was born, she was 18 and came to Bakersfield to help Mom with baby Pete and he had been a favorite of hers ever since.

This Aunt Betty had four sons all big hunks that when they went out for a team, usually made it. Two of them were told to give up their bedroom to us. They could sleep on the living room floor in sleeping bags. I felt terrible about that (tee hee) and Grace felt terrible and guilty (for real). Here she was in a large house with people she had just met, and sleeping in a single bed belonging to one of the boys while missing her parents. She was nineteen and this was the first Christmas away from her parents.

I could tell she was feeling sad and not asleep. I asked, "Would you like to joi .. . She was there before I could finish my sentence. I would like to go on record as stating, "If God had wanted us to share a single bed, he would have made one of us smaller. I did not sleep another wink until 2:00 a.m. and lived in fear of falling off the bed.

At 2:00 a.m. I was rescued when young Tom decided it was time for a snack. Grace scooped him up and tiptoed to the kitchen where she had stashed some formula in preparation for the two o'clock feeding. Soon Mark came into the kitchen, followed by Craig, then Steve, then Andy. They sat around and visited while she fed the little critter. Those guys with hearts as big as the rest of their bodies made her feel welcome and loved.

Grace was an only child and growing up she had always wanted a brother or a sister. They made her feel like she had not one, but four big brothers. There was no girls in the Smith family and Grace became their sister in her mind and the Smith family became our favorite place to visit.

On one of these visits a year later, Tommy woke up early and was making noises that we had conditioned ourselves to sleep through. Aunt Betty came in and scooped him up and headed for the kitchen. There, she set him down in the middle of the kitchen. Then she reached for a box of the cereal that goes snap, crackle, and pop and poured half of it in front of the baby. He played with it until we got up. When Grace saw the happy kid and the mess, she apologized and offered to pay for it. Aunt Betty who was also sitting on the floor playing with little one year old Tommy in the cereal. She told Grace it was a cheap baby sitter. I made a mental note to skip breakfast that morning.

Morning was the family Christmas followed by a great breakfast. Then in the afternoon the large house started filling up with more family and friends until it looked like it would split at the seams. It was party, party, party.

To come to the party each person had to bring a wind-up toy. At a pre-arranged time, EVERYONE, crowded into the living room with their wind-up toy and wound them up. On Uncle Wayne's command they were all set free to do their thing. Little wind-up creatures were bounding all over the living room banging cymbals and drums. It was magical. For a few minutes it was chaos, then quiet. When the last toy ran out of energy, the party was over and the good byes began. I can't remember ever having a more special Christmas. I had been treated as an equal by those who had known me since I was a baby. I had a wife and child that I loved and was proud of, and there were no parents, pirates, or parrots telling me what to do.

Maria

I fell in love with Maria the second year we were in Yucca Valley.

Grace had a full-time job with the telephone company, and we had a little money left at the end of the month, so I had time to look and dream.

Maria was a baby blue Ford Econoline window van with the motor cover between the driver and the person in the right-hand seat.

This motor cover served as a table, a seat, and a baby bed when blankets were piled on it. I was disappointed when Ford moved the motor forward. With Minnie the midget car, the capacity to carry any purchases was that of about a large shopping cart.

Maria was brand new, not used, brand new. (At that point, in reality, we probably only owned the glove compartment or some of the sparkplugs and the credit union owned the rest, but in our minds, we were the proud owners of a brand new car.) Did I mention it was brand new. We were so proud we didn't want to stop driving. We so wanted each other to experience the thrill of driving the new car that we kept switching drivers. Some how we found ourselves in Palm Springs instead of Yucca Valley. We didn't care that we missed our goal by 30 miles. We were deliriously happy.

"We need to do something to celebrate," I said.

Grace agreed.

"What do you want to do?" I asked.

"We could go out to eat."

"Yes, we're in Palm Springs. They have great restaurants here according to Reeves. What do you want?" (I didn't really have to ask.)

"Cheeseburger."

"Sigh."

"Double-decker with a Pepsi and fries."

We passed one of their fancy theaters. It was showing "The Sound of Music" with Julie Andrews. I remembered my Aunt Elizabeth saying if she could only see one movie again the rest of her life it would be "The Sound of Music."

"Hey Grace, I hear they have great cheeseburgers here," I lied. They didn't. But they had the greatest movie in the nicest environment that I could ever remember seeing and gourmet popcorn. Everything was so good we were almost speechless. (I was; she wasn't.)

On the drive home, Grace said, "Do you know what we should name our car?"

"Cheeseburger?" I guessed. (We had stopped at a burger restaurant afterwards.)

"No silly. We should name her Maria."

That is really clever I thought: *Maria **Von Trapp** gave Grace the idea for naming the van Maria Van Wheatley.* For the next 900,000 miles she was called Maria for short.

Maria was a wonderful vehicle. She was with us for over ten years and thousands and thousands of miles. She served us well and took us over and through countless adventures.

By The Time I Get To Phoenix

Sarge and Donna were in tall cotton. Sarge had a good job with Turpens and Donna was a teacher for the pre-school over the hill and across from the boarding school.

Twice a winter they invited us to meet them in Phoenix. It was approximately halfway and allowed them to get away from the snow and see their daughter and grandchild. It allowed us to stay with people we love, in a fancy motel, and eat out.

We would leave Yucca Valley as soon as school got out and start driving to Phoenix. It was approximately a six-hour drive not counting bathroom stops, and we would be heading into Phoenix about eleven at night. At that time the interstate was not completed and we lost interstate conditions around Glendale or Peoria.

I remember on one occasion we were about fifteen minutes from our goal at eleven p.m. and listening to the radio, when they played a new song I had never heard before. It still has the power to take me back to that very moment over fifty years ago. It is "By the Time I Get to Phoenix" sung by Glen Campbell.

Petrarch and Laura

Petrarch our Boxer was a great puppy and a pretty good dog until the babies started coming. I think he may have been jealous of them. When we were at work he would contentedly stay in the backyard sleeping or playing with his favorite toy, a 16-pound bowling ball. He and I would go for long walks in the desert or I would let him chase me on the motorcycle. (He wasn't the one on the motorcycle, I was.) Back in those days, there was more space than people in Yucca Valley.

Our babysitter's husband was a disagreeable old cuss who I will call Ivan, as in Ivan the Terrible. He owned a pretty little female Boxer named Laura that he wanted to breed to Petrarch. I turned him down several times. Then he offered to pay me. I said, "NO."

He offered to pay more. I didn't trust him. I said, "No."

He offered to pay in advance.

I said, "Show me the money." He did.

I made one last attempt to get out of any deal and said,. "I get pick of the litter also." I didn't get out of the deal. Ivan accepted.

I named the puppy Chip because he was a chip off the old block, blox, bloxer, Boxer. Hee hee Sometimes I just slay me... But, I'm getting ahead of myself.

When Laura came in heat I walked my dog the quarter mile down the sandy desert road to his house. There were several mongrels hanging around; Ivan was in the front yard throwing rocks and sticks at them. We locked both Laura and Petrarch in the garage together. Then I walked home.

The next morning when I went to pick up my dog, Ivan demanded his money back. According to him, nothing happened. He said every time he went out to the garage to check on them, Petrarch was sleeping on one side of the garage and Laura was on the other side sleeping or walking back and forth trying to entice him. Ivan said he had to keep waking Petrarch up by banging on a pot with a stick. He said I had a queer dog. (His word and not mine.) with Narcolepsy. (His word, not mine.) I looked it up when I got home. It is a sleeping disease. I told Ivan his dog must be pig ugly in the dog world or likely had a preference for dogs of her own gender or preferred that riff-raff that had been hanging around. I tried to think of something to balance his fancy Narcolepsy comment.

"And your dog, probably has . . . has . . . Chicken Pox." (I think I lost that one.) We finally came to a compromise. I would let his dog have one more visit for free the next weekend.

I suspect the old guy must have doused his dog with some kind of French canine perfume or love potion. There must have been a hot time in the old barn (garage) that night. There was no need to bang the pot with a stick. Every time Ivan checked on them, they were . . . dancing. (My word, not his.)

When I went to get Petrarch, he wouldn't come when I called him, and I had to drag him all the way home. (It was a quarter-mile tug-of-war.) I was exhausted when we reached home and had no more than locked him in the backyard when he got a running start and sailed over the top of a six-foot fence. I was not in the mood nor had the energy to go after him.

It wasn't five minutes before our phone started ringing. "Your dog is down here scratching the Hell out of my garage door."

"Well, the horse's fanny," I said.

"COME AND GET HIM," he demanded.

"No, I'm mad at him right now. We aren't speaking. Ivan didn't say anything. He had emphysema and was having trouble catching his breath.

You can have him for the whole weekend," I said generously and hung up while he was trying to catch his breath. Thirty seconds later, the phone rang. I ignored it. Grace picked it up and said, "It's for you."

Gasp. "I don't want your damn dog for the whole weekend!"

"Who is this?"

" I'm going to call the dog catcher. Your dog is a sex maniac."

"I'm not sure Yucca Valley has a dog catcher. And be sure to point out that you don't have a license for your dog, or do you want me to tell him?"

He thought about that for a minute then countered with, "Do you want Alice to keep babysitting for you?"

I did. She was a very good babysitter and charged us below the going rate. I went down to drag Petrarch back home for the second time. Riff and Raff were nowhere to be seen. I have to admit, I took some pleasure when I saw the scratch marks on his garage door. I figured Laura must have been moved to the house because Petrarch was now trying to break into it, and the front door was starting to look like the garage door. I noticed Petrarch was cut up and he had been bleeding. "What did you do to my dog?"

"Nothing. He got that when he was escorting Riff and Raff off the property. He's pretty strong. They did not want to go at first;" he continued.

I put the leash on Petrarch and started for home. It was another epic tug-of-war. When we got home, I tied the end of Petrarch's long leash to some lawn furniture in the backyard. That was a mistake. This time he didn't soar over the top of the fence. He went through it. The bamboo was no match for true love. The lawn furniture hung up when it got to the fence and was still in the yard attached to his leash, and he was on the other side of the hole howling his heart out.

Ivan got a nice batch of puppies which he sold for a profit. And I got Chip, who I had to sell to replace a section of fence and a piece of outdoor furniture. I figure that little adventure cost me about fifty dollars.

Ringy Dingy Dingy

Time flew by. Baby Tom was a delight and everyone loved him. Grace and I were newlyweds more in love with each other every day.

The telephone company came to town and put in a call center. They were going to need operators and they wanted people who lived in the area. They offered three weeks of classes down in San Bernardino. For most of them a motel and free food was included, but Grace and one other made the hour drive down and back every day so they could spend a few waking moments with their families. For them, the use of a company car was provided. Many found the classes hard and dropped out. Grace thought they were easy and came out top in the class.

It wasn't long before our family consisted of one teacher, one telephone operator, a Boxer, and the neatest little kid in California.

As an operator Grace was working split shifts 10 to 2 and 6 to 10 and there were a lot of weekends and holidays she had to work. When a supervisor couldn't make it, it was Grace who took her place and did an excellent job. When an opening came up for a permanent supervisor she applied for it.

She was told it wouldn't look good to have a 19-year-old in charge and they told her she wasn't eligible because of her age. Grace asked if there was any other job she was eligible for. She was ready to quit.

They told her they needed someone in the service center to route the technicians and repairmen. The job was five days a week, 8 to 5, no split shifts, no weekends, and no holidays. It was the answer to our prayers, or as my father would say, "a bird's nest on the ground."

It allowed us to plan things like visiting relatives on weekends and going on sails to Catalina.

Baby D. J.

We decided to have another baby when Tom was nearing two. He was such a good baby, we felt we owed it to the world to bring forth another. My brother and I were just a little over two years apart and we thought this was a successful period of time as it allowed us to share many adventures growing up.

All caution and protection was thrown to the wind and it wasn't too long before Grace announced, "We're going to have a baby."

She called to make an appointment to see Dr. A., the doctor who had delivered Tom. There was a longer than normal pause after Grace identified herself. We were both so healthy (and broke) we had not seen Dr. A since a couple of visits after Tom's birth.

His receptionist asked what the problem was, and Grace said, "No problem. We are going to have a baby." She was smiling as she said it.

"I'm sorry Mrs. Wheatley, the doctor no longer takes obstetrics cases."

"How long has this been going on?" Grace asked. "He delivered my firstborn."

"When was that?"

"Not quite two years ago."

"Oh! You're **that** Mrs. Wheatley. I believe you might have been his last case," she said diplomatically "I hear lots of good things about Dr. B. You might try his office."

Grace signed up with Dr. B and was quite happy with him. However, she wondered if she might be partially responsible for Dr. A. giving up obstetrics, then dismissed the idea as being ridiculous.

Months passed. Then came the day. The day when Grace announced, "It's time." She did not have to tell me what it was time for. It was **not** "Time For Beany" or "Howdy Doody Time." (Two popular children's shows with puppets when I was a child.)

I was nervous, but not anything like the first time. I was somewhere between a 5 and a 10 on the nervous scale.

Grace phoned the doctor's office, but no one was there. All she got was a busy signal. We realized it was a weekend. (My score went up ten points on the nervous scale.) Grace phoned the hospital and asked them to get in touch with Dr. B. They told her he was playing in a golf tournament in Palm Springs and suggested she sit in a warm bathtub and meditate. (I gained another ten points on the scale.)

Grace gave it a shot. For half an hour she sat in a bathtub full of warm water going "AHMMM." But the baby wasn't cooperating. It wanted out of there. Grace came out of the bathroom and announced, "No 'ands' 'ifs' or 'buts.' That baby **is** coming today. And it **will** happen at the hospital even if it is on top of the front desk." (I just blasted through 80% on the nervous scale. The picture that statement conjured up in my mind was not a pretty one.

When we got to the hospital everyone was skeptical. Grace had made history with the birth of Tom and . . . her ability to be heard as far away as Joshua Tree. She was legend. Then there was the little incident of the false pregnancy and before that, the husband who watched a birth through the reflection on a medical cabinet.

They did not put much stock in our opinions on things medical. **But** . . .

But the woman who walked into the hospital that day was not the timid eighteen-year-old of her last visit. This woman was not anyone to ignore. She had supervised and survived a gaggle of female telephone operators and telephone repairmen as well as the ride from Big Bear to Yucca Valley by way of Pioneer Town. This **was** the niece of Long John Auntie and the daughter of Sergeant (Short-tempered) Cousins.

Grudgingly a nurse took Grace into an examining room after she threatened to climb up on the reception desk and have the baby.. I could tell the nurse was nervous about being alone in the room with this crazy woman. I was holding baby Tom who was crying, and I was on the verge of joining him myself. He had never seen his mother like this, nor had I. I soared through the 90s on the nervous scale and was in uncharted territory.

The nurse came running back and shouted, "Stat. Get the doctor. The baby is **crowning**." I had never heard that term before. Maybe I had misheard her. Then the nurse said, "I don't know why she didn't come in sooner."

I was glad that Grace was in a different room and didn't hear that. If she had, there might have been a bald-headed nurse.

"The reason she didn't come in sooner, Miss Smarty Pants, was she was taking a bath," I said. "Like someone from this hospital told her to do over the phone." The nurse's face turned red; I am guessing she might have been the one Grace had been talking to on the phone."

Baby Tommy nodded and said "Bath AHMMM."

"Did they say the baby is **drowning**?" I asked the man standing behind me holding some packages.

"Crowning," he said.

"**They** . . . were the ones who told her to go sit in a bathtub. I'm going to sue."

"Good idea." said the man with the packages. "With all those packages, you almost look like a UPS man?" I joked.

"I am a UPS man."

"Oh."

"Would you sign for these packages for me?"

"NO!"

All this place needs is a Cheshire Cat, I thought.

In through the front door strode the doctor. He did not look particularly happy. He recognized me and looked particularly unhappy. (The doctors and hospital had some kind of agreement that one of them would be on call every fourth weekend. This weekend was his turn to cover any emergencies. It was not Dr. B. the golfer. It was Dr. A, the doctor who Grace had driven out of obstetrics.

"Have you remarried," he asked hopefully. I shook my head.

Everything went well after that. Grace said it was over before she knew it and a smiling Dr. A. even agreed to take care of all post-birth visits.

There was only one thing left for me to do that night, phone back to New Mexico and bring them up to date on the situation. (Grace had phoned back there earlier in the day when everything was going wrong, asking for suggestions.) They were all huddled around the phone awaiting news.

My call was answered on the first ring by the mother.

"Guess who this is."

"Telemarketer."

"No, it's your favorite son-in-law."

"Don't have one."

"Cut the crap," called Auntie from somewhere in the room.

"Cut the crap," called the parrot.

I started out by saying, "I've got some bad news." I heard a lot of groaning in the background. "I think you all better sit down for this." (More groans) "Terrible news. I added."

I heard someone say, "OH DEAR."

"Are you all sitting down?"

"Yes," said Big Donna.

"Yes," said the sarge.

"Yes," said Uncle Bob.

"Yes," said Aunt Betty.

"Hell No," said Auntie.

"Hell No," said the parrot.

"Okay, buckle up. (I cleared my throat.) It is my sad duty to . . . (I stopped and started over with a quiver in my voice for effect.) I regret to inform you that . . . (I paused for even more effect.) . . . "IT'S A . . . GIRL."

I'm sorry, but I can't repeat some of the clever comments I heard next from Sarge, Big Donna, Auntie and the parrot. Nobody thought I was funny.

Oops, I almost forgot to tell you. We named the baby girl Donna Jean Wheatley after her two grandmothers, even though she acted more like Auntie the Terrible.

(You may have noticed that I started calling my mother-in-law Big Donna. She officially became Big Donna when the baby, Little Donna, was born. I guess if Grace (Donna Grace) hadn't used her middle name, she would have been known as middle Donna.)

So far there have been no babies named after me and I am in my 80s. It's not looking too good for my chances. I did get an honorable mention with a family named Bitsilly. They named one of their boys Barry Grant (Hooray), but they call him Barry (Boo). Oh yes, many years later, my daughter named her last child Grant. (Hip Hip Hooray) James Grant. (Hooray.)They call him James (Boo).

This new baby was Tom's opposite in every way. Smile, chuckle, and grin were not in her vocabulary. Hers consisted of eat, poop, sleep, and cry. I called her Donna Jean Sourpuss for the first three years of her life.

Another thing about this new baby. She was bald. And she stayed bald for the whole first years of her life. Grace started taping ribbons to her bald head because people kept saying things like, "What a handsome baby. How old is **he**?" "Is it a boy or a girl?" "My baby had a full head of hair the day he was born."

The day after Little Donna was born I took Tom with me on a visit to see his mother. At the end of the visit, I took him down to the baby viewing window to see his sibling. There were only two babies. You may have heard of love at first sight. I pointed her out and told Tom she and his mother would be going home with us the next day.

He looked at me and said "NO. That one." He wanted the one with hair that was not crying.

"That works for me," I said. Unfortunately the other parents and Grace were party poopers.

I phoned Mom and Dad to let them know the world had another Wheatley. Dad was not too excited, but Mom insisted on coming down and helping until Grace was back on her feet, even if it took three weeks. I think it bugged her that it had been Big Donna who had helped when Tom was born. I picked Mom up at the Palm Springs airport the next day.

Mom was a tremendous help and she fell in love with the high desert. I don't think she wanted to leave the land of sunshine for the land of rain. Her phone conversations and letters with Dad went from "when are you coming home," to "come home," to her receiving airplane tickets in the mail for the next day. It was a sad moment for us watching her walk out towards the plane that would take her to Los Angeles (LAX) where she would catch the plane for Seattle (SEA).

At school I told everyone there was a new baby in the Wheatley family. Mrs. Duval asked when they'd get to see the baby. I said just as soon as Grace gets out of the hospital.

"When will that be?" asked Mrs. Jessup.

"Two or three days," I said. I wasn't really anxious to show off this baldheaded baby with the bad attitude. Tom had been such a perfect baby, I didn't want to show that we weren't able to make another perfect baby.

"Two or three days," scoffed Mrs. Lofgren. "These modern women are a bunch of tulips. Why when I felt my fifth child was coming, I got off the tractor, walked up to the house, delivered her, made a sandwich, and in less than an hour I was back on the tractor, and I finished the south forty before the sun went down."

I couldn't top that. I think I said that Grace hadn't been feeling well and the staying in the hospital was the doctor's idea.

"Tulips," said Mrs. Lofgren

Mrs. Jessup came to my rescue. "Lofgren, what do you want them to do, buy a tractor? And you mean you actually stopped your plowing and took a whole hour off. Why when my last child was born . . . "

I hurried from the room. The last thing I wanted to know about was the gory details. I didn't hear most of the rest because I was out the door in a jiffy, maybe half a jiffy. Would that be a jif? But I did hear, just before the door to the teacher's lounge closed, Mrs. Jessup's voice saying, "fifteen minutes." And I thought to myself, *around here, the first liar doesn't have a chance.*

Time to Go

After three years they offered me tenure. I would gladly have stayed, but Grace needed to finish college. She wanted a Bachelor of Science with a specialty in Home Economics.

We researched and learned the three top colleges in Home Ec. were located in Salem, San Diego, and Fort Collins.

I wrote to the school systems in all three cities. I was hoping for San Diego because it was the closest, and California Schools paid the most. However, the only school system that would interview me on a weekend was in Colorado. AND I was not about to take time off from the school district and valley that had been so good to us to apply for another job on company time.

That is why on one Friday night after school, I got in my car and drove to LA International Airport, and caught a plane to Denver. It was near midnight when I rented the cheapest car Avis had and traveled north to Fort Collins. An hour later I checked in at the first open motel I came to.

My appointment was at ten in the morning at Dunn Elementary with a Mr. Ray Hayden who was the principal. There was already another applicant there ahead of me when I arrived. We were both early and had a chance to visit. I liked James Arthur a lot. He had a great personality and 10 years more experience than I, not to mention several outstanding teacher awards.

I had none. He was called in first. The door did not close completely and I could hear the questions and answers. I started taking notes thinking I might even use a few of his answers. It sounded like Mr. Arthur and Mr. Hayden were really bonding and on the same page in all areas. Both men were smiling when James Arthur came out. Mr. Hayden said, "You will be hearing from me soon, James."

When I went in for my turn, Mr. Hayden looked up from the papers I had filled out, including references from others. Mr. Hayden did not look all that friendly like he had with Mr. Arthur.

I stuck out my hand and said I would like to thank you and the Poudre School District for allowing me to interview on a weekend. I pronounced the school district as pow-tree.

He said, "Your welcome and it's pronounced pooh-der." He paused for about thirty seconds. I couldn't tell what he was thinking. He did not look like the happy person he been when interviewing James Arthur. "I nearly didn't agree to interview you because of this." He handed me a paper. He had circled something on it in red ink. Actually, several somethings. The paper looked like it was bleeding. It reminded me of some of my high school papers.

"If it's about room environment and bulletin boards, I'm getting better and my wife comes in and helps me on weekends."

"Read," he said.

It was from my current principal, Mr.(Good Lord Cried the Woodchuck) Milligan. Principal Marvin had moved on up to the mid school. It said, "The biggest thing I have against Mr. Wheatley is he doesn't support his professional organizations."

I admitted I was the only teacher in the whole school district that did not join all three organizations. And yes, I knew it did give our school a black mark in the eyes of some.

"What possible justification can you give for this unprofessional behavior?" he growled.

I quoted Shakespeare's Hamlet, "To thine own self be true. Then it must follow as the night the day that thou canst not be false to any man." I was not sure of the relevance or if I was even quoting correctly, but people are often impressed with things Shakespeare wrote.

I could tell by the expression on his face that he wasn't one of these people. The expression on his face was telling me he was thinking *what kind of nut do I have here? We can't let him near any of our kids.*

I decided to give the truth a shot and told him that Ronald Regan and Pat Brown were running for governor of California, and after studying both men, I believed Ronald Regan would be a better governor than Pat Brown, and the CTA (California Teachers Association) was pouring lots of money collected from its members' dues to Brown's campaign. And I told him the MTA (the local Morongo Teachers Association) would not let a teacher join it if they didn't join the other two.

Mr. Hayden said, "This interview is over." I thought, *Alas poor Wheatley, I knew him well, Horatio.*

As I reached the door, he called out. "Just a second. There is one other thing on this paper you should probably read."

He pointed to two sentences scribbled in the bottom margin. They were underlined and said, "If you don't want Wheatley, send him back. Tell him I have not turned in his letter of resignation yet."

I thanked Mr. Hayden and excused myself. It was a long sad drive to the Denver airport, and the flight wasn't any better. All I could think about was the money and time I had wasted. It was great to see my little car all shiny waiting for me in the long-distance parking. I'm surprised I did not get lost or in an accident. It was getting dark and LA traffic is scary and complicated with people zooming in and out and around. Also, a large portion of my mind was trying to figure out how I was going to break the news to Grace.

A couple of hours later, Grace saw the little car turn in the driveway. She had been watching for me for the last forty-five minutes and came out to welcome me home. Grace had dressed up for the returning hero and looked so good. She was holding baby Donna who miraculously was not crying, and holding little Tommy's hand. He too was dressed up for Daddy's triumphant return. We had a group hug, with nobody speaking for over a minute. Then I stepped back and said, "I have some bad news."

"Me too," she said.

"WHAT?" My troubles were immediately forgotten. "WELL?" I demanded after she didn't speak.

"Perhaps you'd better sit down."

"No, just tell me what happened."

"Not until you sit down."

We walked into the living room, and I sat down on the couch. "Okay, now tell me."

She handed me the **sleeping** baby, which explained why there was no crying. "IT'S A GIRL," she said. For a minute the room was deathly quiet. Then she started chanting, "Got Cha, Got Cha, Cha Cha Cha," as she danced around the room. Little Tommy tried to imitate some of her moves and sing along.

I didn't know whether to laugh, give her a punch, or cry. I wasn't used to having my own jokes thrown back in my face. I did none of the above. Then reality set in. I still had to tell her my bad news, and it wasn't funny.

I waited until dance time was over, then I spoke. "Even worse than your sorry joke," I said. "Mr. Hayden, the man I went to see . . . "

"I know," She said solemnly. He phoned this afternoon with the news."

I went on to explain. "It was the not joining all the professional organizations thing, plus there was this really neat guy applying for the same position."

Grace smiled. "He said to tell you the job is yours and the contract is in the mail."

I was stunned. It was a good thing I was sitting down.

A week later we heard from the college. Grace had been accepted, and we would be staying in Aggie Village which was the college's married student housing.

I mention all that to mention this. Pets were not allowed in Aggie Village. Petrarch's days as a Wheatley were numbered.

Even without the Aggie Village excuse. I knew it would happen ever since, in a playful mood, Petrarch grabbed the table cloth and gave it a jerk. Twelve baby bottles Grace had just sanitized and were air drying on the table crashed to the kitchen floor.

The Rescue

Two problems arose. The first was the California schools ran on a different timetable than the Colorado schools. For Grace to restart her educational pursuit of a degree with the summer session she would have to be there before my job ended.

They would probably have let me go early, but Wheatley's aren't like that. If they say they will do something, like honoring a contract, they will do it or die trying.

The school district allowed the teachers ten paid sick days a year. It is amazing to me how many of the teachers were sick exactly ten days a year. I left after three years with28 sick days not used.

The next problem was how were we going to get our stuff to Fort Collins? We had moved to Yucca Valley with everything (all our belongings) in a borrowed station wagon. To leave we would need to rent a U-Haul and one of us would have to tow the Metropolitan (Minnie) with the van (Maria).

Grace's classes and the end of my teaching assignment overlapped. If Grace drove the U-Haul, she wouldn't have transportation in Fort Collins for 2 weeks unless she towed one of our vehicles, which she absolutely refused to do. She said she had never driven a big truck or towed anything and it would mean she'd be heading off into the desert with a baby and a two year old. Too many things could go wrong. If she drove the van she'd be short of things to run a house containing two little kids, and I'd be stuck loading most of our belongings by myself and towing the Metro.

The plan we decided on was Grace would drive Maria and carry everything she could. I would drive the U-Haul and tow the Metro.

I went down and reserved a U-Haul truck for two weeks from then. When I got back to the house there was a strange pick-up in the driveway. I wondered, *who can that be? We can't be entertaining anyone, we have work to do.*

Out of the house came Cousin Ed followed by the sarge. "We've come to help you move," one of them said. I phoned the U-Haul people and asked, "That truck I reserved for two weeks from now, can I get it sooner?"

"Sure. When do you want it?"

"Half an hour."

We spent the rest of the day loading all our belongings in the U-Haul, Ed's truck, and Maria. It was back-breaking work. I was amazed: we had moved out to California with all our belongings in a borrowed station wagon and now it took two trucks and a van to move us. Exhausted, we went to Kenny's motel.

We were all tired, and sweaty from the loading, so we took showers and dressed up to eat at a nice restaurant. I believe it was called The Glen. Grace gave the baby bottle to our waiter and asked if he would have the kitchen warm it up for her.

We were in an earnest conversation about the best possible route when the baby bottle was returned. Grace absent-mindedly started shaking the bottle so it would drip on her forearm, to make sure it was not too hot for the baby. But she and the rest of us were so engrossed in the conversation she failed to notice she was missing her arm and the formula was going into a pocket of Ed's new suit which, he was very proud of. (This may have been the first time he ever wore it.)

Grace was the first to notice, Ed was the second. A pocket full of warm baby formula is not in the same class or as desirable as a pocket full of rainbows. In his haste to get the coat off, he spilled it on his pants making a stain that looked like he might have trouble containing his water. I've heard that no good deed goes unpunished. This was an excellent example of that statement.

The next morning bright and early, I watched the little caravan head east. It would be two weeks before I could join my family. They would go as far as the ranch the first day and then on to Fort Collins on the second day, a total distance of twelve hundred miles.

My back was killing me from loading all our belongings. The sarge and Grace were hurting more than I was. Ed and I worked together and handled the heaviest stuff. Ed was the only one who seemed unscathed if you don't count the damage to his suit.

I was feeling guilty knowing they would be one man short when they were unloading. And it got worse. When they got there, they received some good news and some bad news. The good news was the apartment was right next to the fenced-in play yard for kids with swings, slides, and monkey bars. The bad news was the apartment was on the second floor. Everything had to be carried up a flight of stairs.

"Phone your husband, I bet he'll tell us to hire some locals to move your stuff upstairs," suggested the sarge, after he saw the steep steps leading to the second floor. She phoned and told me the situation. "Any humanitarian suggestions," shouted the sarge from the background. "Grace, tell him to lift with his legs, not his back."

Grace said it wasn't long before the sarge's language was becoming more and more colorful. Mothers were rushing to cover their children's ears or taking them to a park or indoors.

She also said the rest periods became longer and longer. An example of the sarge's dialogue went like this.

"Why in the blue Suzie do you and your husband need a couch?" "How many @#$ steps are there?" "Edward, quit pushing so hard?" "I bet that no good son-in-law is lying by a pool in the desert drinking Pina Coladas." "I should have let Auntie kill him." "OH my aching back."

Bye Bye Boxer

I tried to **sell** Petrarch to Ivan, Sarge, Big Donna, Long John Auntie, Bob & Betty, my parents, my brother, my principal, anyone, and the parrot. There were no takers. I tried to **give** him away to Ivan, Sarge, Big Donna, Long John Auntie, Bob & Betty, my parents, my brother, my principal, anyone, and the parrot. There were no takers.

I put an ad in the newspaper.   FREE-

FREE-FREE Three Year Old Boxer: Father, Lover, Bowler, & Champion high jumper.

The ONLY person to answer the ad was a teeny-tiny, sweet, little old lady. She might have weighed 80 pounds soaking wet, and she was 90 if she was a day. I doubted she could control a Chihuahua on a walk. I tried to discourage her. I said he needed a fenced-in yard.

She said she had a fenced-in yard and invited me to come over to see it. She had a lovely large home on an acre of property and the backyard **was** entirely fenced. The fence stood about two feet tall. I think its purpose was to keep out rabbits (short rabbits). Petrarch could jump over it in his sleep, on one leg, blindfolded, even backwards.

But I was up against it timewise. I told her I'd bring him by the next day when I was leaving for Fort Collins. I wanted one last day with my buddy. I hoped he wouldn't die of a broken heart when I left him, and I didn't want her to realize this wasn't a match made in Heaven before I could get out of town.

Even though I didn't want to leave him with her, I rationalized that I knew he wouldn't hurt her, at

FREE-FREE-FREE I wasn't ripping her off; and it gave him a chance for a happy life.

What I feared most might happen was some lovely canine in the valley would come in season, and he would pack his bag and go. It was the sixties and they were playing songs like Glen Campbell's "Gentle On My Mind" on the radio all the time.

On the way to drop him off, I was still considering not stopping and keeping him, when he let loose with a humdinger. Boxers are known for having problems with gas. Even James Heriot directed a chapter to this problem in one of his books. My eyes were watering so much I could hardly see and I pulled over to the side of the road and jumped out of the car. It took me a couple of minutes to get all the windows down and stop coughing and gagging.

He sat there on the passenger seat with a proud, happy smile on his face that seemed to be saying, "I feel much better and what's your problem?"

There is no way I would be able to be cooped up in that small space for 1200 miles enduring those zephyrs. The decision to leave him became etched in stone.

When I dropped him off, I suggested she keep him in the house for about four hours. I figured I could be past Blythe by then and in Arizona safe from California jurisdiction.

As I walked him up to her house, I noticed something smelled really good. "What is that smell?" I asked.

"I'm making my new friend a casserole for his lunch." She bent over and gave him a kiss on the top of the head. "What is his favorite meal?" she asked.

"Pheasant under glass," I joked. She actually wrote it down. I hate it when I try to be funny and people think I am serious.

"Anything else you can think of?"

I decided to give it one more try. "Roadkill rabbit."

She frowned. I noticed she did not write that down. Perhaps she didn't want to have to go out and kill rabbits with her car.

I handed her the leash and ran for the car before he could let loose with a zinger and kill the deal. I drove back to the house and made one last quick sweep to make sure I hadn't left anything.

Then I locked the house and hid the keys in a secret place the landlord had suggested. I hopped into my car and was off to join my wife on another adventure.

It has been over fifty years. I guess it is okay to tell you where the secret hiding place for the keys were: under the foot of the yard gnome.

I was sad about what I was leaving. Yucca Valley had been good, great, and **wonderful** to us. It had given us two children, a great job in an excellent school system, lots of wonderful friends, a new car, reduced debt, and cemented a very happy marriage. I was sad about leaving but excited about what lay ahead.

(Three years later on a vacation trip we stopped by Yucca Valley. I had not been able to get the little old woman and the dog out of my mind. We drove over to her house and rang the bell. She came to the door. I asked if she remembered me.

"No."

I told her I was the one who had given her Petrarch and asked how long he stuck around after I left. She opened the door all the way and pointed.

There was Petrarch lying on the couch watching Jeopardy on television. Well, the television was on, he was on the couch, and the show was Jeopardy. I was truly surprised he was still there. Actually, I was surprised that they both were still there.

I said something about Petrarch and she said, "Oh no, his name is Mama's Baby Boy." She called him over, and he got off the couch and waddled over to stand next to her. He was as wide as he was tall. I thought to myself, *I bet he can't even jump over that back fence now.* I patted him on the head, and he sniffed my hand. I got the feeling that he recognized me. I saw the same body language and the same look come into his eyes and body that I had seen when I was pulling him away from the garage door of his lady love three years earlier.

As we walked away Grace said, "Something sure smelled good." I looked at my watch. It was after six. "It must be time for Mama's Baby Boy's supper," I said.

Disneyland Birthday

Desert Christ Park

Yucca Valley house on the Hill

First day of school

Classroom one weak (sic) before school

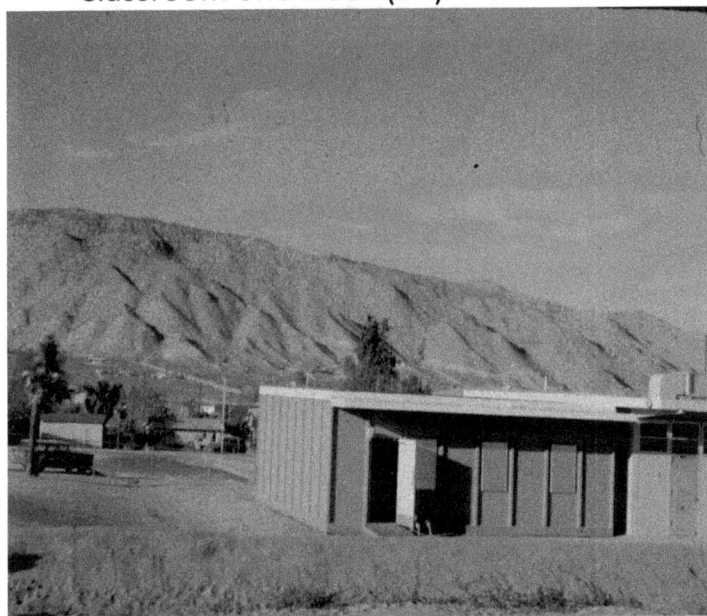

Classroom in place on time

Pullups
"27, 28, 29, 30"

Tommy's first Christmas tree

Smith Christmas AM

Smith Christmas PM

Little Fish/Old People

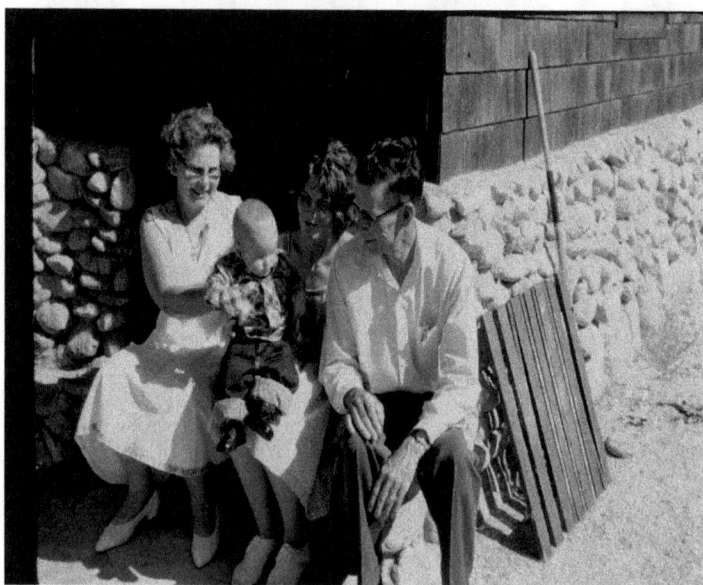

Donna, Tom, Grace & Sarge

Flying baby

Tommy

"Look at the birdy."
"Not that birdy Charley."

Manager Reeves and Coach Wheatley

Bye Bye Boxer

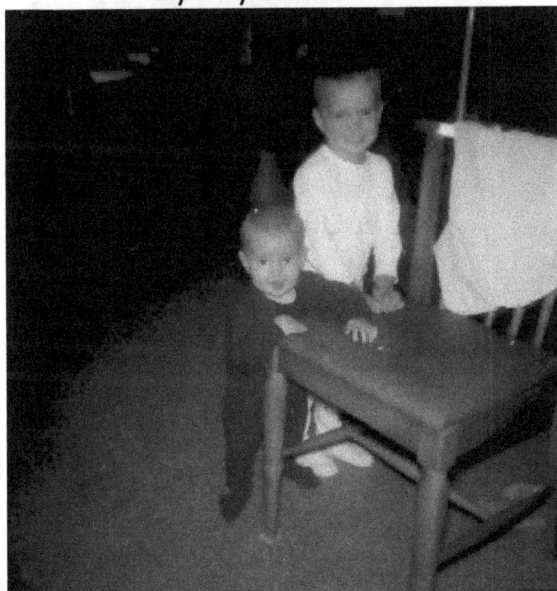

Little Donna & Big Tom

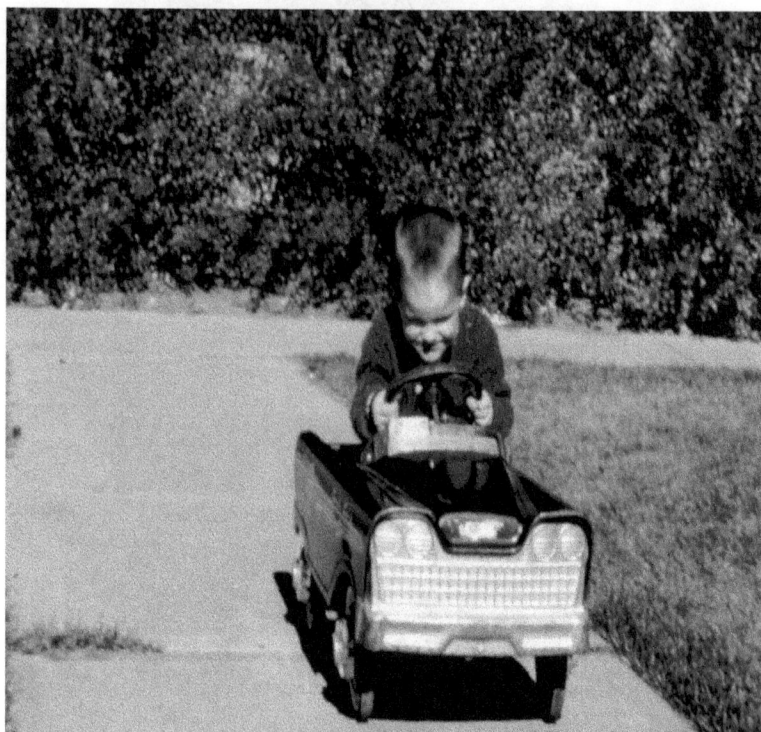

"Get Out of my Way!"

BOOK THREE

Colorado Again

Wild Bill

I was introducing myself and shaking hands with the other teachers in the teacher's lounge when I first heard about Bill.

"Hello, my name is Pete Wheatley. I am the new 5th Grade teacher," I said to a little lady. Her friendly smile vanished and was replaced with a look of concern for me.

"Oh, you poor dear," said the lady at the other end of my arm. "You will have Wild Bill in your class. I had him last year. See these gray hairs? They weren't there last year when school started." Several of the other teachers slowly shook their heads. They all had Bill stories.

It turns out that Bill was the reason I got the job in Fort Collins. The week before school started, Mr. Hayden called me into his office and told me about one of the early families in the area.

He said Bill came from this stock and was living with his father who often drank too much and last year Bill was starting to rebel.

He told me Bill was smart, had a great personality, and needed to be helped back on the right track.

Mr. Hayden went on to say, "I figured anyone who is stubborn enough to stand up to a whole school district by himself, might be the one Bill needs. Anyone who had the confidence to fly out from Los Angeles on the possibility of applying for the only job available, might be the one who would get through to Bill."

This was the first I had heard that it was this job or nothing. I felt sick. But I did not try to correct this misconception on his part. There is no way I would spend the money and time to fly halfway across the country for a single chance at a job.

Mr. Hayden continued. "I phoned down to Fort Lewis to see if anyone remembered you. I was told you might be the clown that climbed up the side of the dorm to wash the outside windows of his second-story dorm room."

I didn't actually lie. I just didn't deny or confirm the accusation. You might remember I had promised to quit telling falsehoods. I shook my head and said, "That would be a silly thing for anyone to do."

Mr. Hayden continued. "And one of the dorm proctors claims it was your footprints on the hall ceiling and there was something about an incident in the school library. Even though I hated to turn Mr. Arthur down, I think you would be the perfect fit for Bill."

There were many confrontations between Bill and me. I was not sure if I was making any progress or not, but I really liked the kid and could see the great potential in him. Perhaps I was too close to the forest, but by Thanksgiving some of the talk in the teacher's lounge were things like "Have you noticed the change in Bill?" (They didn't have to say Bill who.)

The small teacher with the gray hair shared that she was carrying a big load of books down the hall when Bill offered to carry them for her. She said, "He was very **charming,**"

I couldn't help myself; I sang, "Could he bake a cherry pie, this Charming Billy?"
I really liked this young man and enjoyed our time together both during and after school.

However, the following year I was just a teacher in his rearview mirror, one he had had when he was a kid; he had out-grown me, but I kept hearing good reports and when no one was looking, Bill would occasionally stick his head inside the door to my class and wink or say, "How are things, Mr. Wheatley?"

Chatty Kathy

A. J. Dunn Elementary was only 10 blocks from where we would be staying in Aggie Village: married student housing. I could shave even more blocks off that by cutting straight across campus. Rather than fire up a vehicle for such a short distance, I decided to buy a bicycle. Mr. Hayden told me the police were having a bike auction on Wednesday.

Tuesday night was my first PTA meeting in my new town. Part of the meeting was introducing the new teachers and encouraging the parents to get to know the new teachers after the meeting. There were only a couple of us. Dunn was such a great school, teachers did not want to leave.

I met a zillion people that night, a trillion of which were concerned young mothers bent on telling me their life story with emphasis on child-raising concerns. (Did I ever mention that math was not . . . something.) We didn't get out of the building until almost eleven.

The next day, I arrived late to the auction because Bill had been acting up in class, and I kept him after school. Then I had to drive him home. The auction was a quarter over when I arrived. One of the young mothers yelled a greeting to me as I walked by her.

Hello again," she called out. She had 2 children standing beside her and one in a stroller. Nice looking well behaved children. It looked like they were within a year of each other. *This woman must be a virtual baby-making machine* I thought. She looked familiar, and I was madly trying to remember which of the trillion she was, from the PTA meeting the night before. I had it narrowed down to the dentist's wife, a member of the school board, the PTA secretary, or one of the other trillion. (What's a trillion minus three?)

I could not remember any of their names, so I just yelled back a generic, "Hello Again," following her lead and kept on walking to where I could get a better look at what was being auctioned. I hoped she would stay where she was so I wouldn't embarrass myself by not knowing her name.

No such luck. The four of them ambled over to where I was standing. She started talking to me about her husband: that he was buying a bike so he could ride it to school and let her have the car; that he was studying to be a veterinarian; he was in his second year; the different things he, she and the kids were doing, etc., etc. The place was packed, and I wasn't able to spot her husband who was in the front row.

She chatted on merrily, but I missed most of what she said because I was concentrating on the bikes being put up to bid on, while still trying to be polite in case she was the school board member, and pretending to be listening to what she was saying.

I bid on several of the bicycles but that didn't earn me any wheels. Most I bid on went for double my highest bid. I finally decided I would rather get my bicycle from the Schwinn store. That way if anything went wrong, it would be backed by a warranty. I decided to leave.

I turned to the woman to excuse myself, while thinking, *does this woman ever stop to inhale?* All of the sudden she said, "Oops, gotta go. Looks like we just bought a bike, and I've got the family checkbook. Nice seeing you again Jacks."

Jacks?" Chatty Kathy thought I was someone else. Someone called Jack, whose last name started with an "S." Or was she calling me a jack-ess. (If that was the case, she needed to buy a vowel and another "s") It doesn't look bad in print, but I don't like the way Jack S. sounds. I shouldn't be too critical; I had done the same thing and thought she was someone else. She definitely wasn't the dentist's wife, board member, or the secretary of the PTA. I was feeling sorry for this husband of hers.

Sounded like she ruled the roost. She had the checkbook and she was going to have the car while his transportation would be a used stolen bicycle bought at a police auction.

Then it dawned on me. My wife was the keeper of the checkbook and she was driving our best vehicle, and I had been checking out stolen bicycles at a police auction. Kathy's husband and I might have a lot more in common than I first thought.

I shook my head as I walked to where my car was parked a block away. Chatty Kathy and Bill had probably prevented me from saving a lot of money on a bicycle. When I got to my car I noticed someone had pulled up too close behind me, and I had parked too close to the car in front of me. I decided the car behind me had been driven by a Honyok. (Rube or simpleton) I, however, was not a Honyok because the space in front of the car in front of me was protected by being the entrance to a driveway and that car could not be blocked in.

"Well Minnie, I said to my little car, "I haven't seen you in this tight a spot since New Year's 65."

But it wasn't as bad as New Year's 65, and I was soon back on the road heading for Aggie Village. Maria, our Ford Econoline van was Grace's to use because Minnie was too small for Grace and the kids, not because I wasn't the boss.

I turned on the radio. Don Gibson was just finishing "Oh Lonesome Me." The next song was by Johnny Cash. Fort Collins was excited because Johnny was coming to town in a couple of weeks. We already had our tickets to his show: down in front, 4th row back.

Included on the show were his brother Tommy, wife June, Carl Perkins, the Statler Brothers, and the Tennessee Two (or Three; I am not too good at math). The song they were playing on the radio was "Jackson." Johnny had recorded it with his wife June. Suddenly I snapped off the radio. A thought had struck me like a bolt of lightning. Could Chatty Kathy have been saying, "Nice seeing you again, *Jackson?*"

Only one person had ever called me that. *It couldn't be her! Could it be her?* If it was, no wonder she seemed so familiar. Recognition exploded into my brain as I identified so many of Mary's mannerisms in Chatty Kathy. Yes, it was her! It had to be her. I couldn't believe it. I had talked to her (Translation: listened to her.) for 20 minutes and had not recognized her.

Back in Fort Lewis days when I was trying to resist her, I had pictured her putting on weight in future years. Chatty Kathy had actually gone in the other direction. This woman was thin, probably the result of trying to repopulate the planet with her own private baby boom.

Twenty minutes had passed and I was almost home, but I whipped the car into a U-turn and drove back to the auction. I was able to park closer because many had gone, unfortunately, that included Kathy (Mary) and her family. I just wanted to get a peek at who she had married. I hoped it was the one I called the mystery man. She had seemed so happy with him that last trimester at Fort Lewis.

A couple of days later in the morning before her eleven o'clock Friday class, Grace had finished cleaning the apartment and was dirty and sweating to an exercise program designed to help ladies regain their shape after childbirth when there came a knock on the door.

When she opened the door expecting one of the neighbors, there stood Mary, the last person on earth Grace wanted to see when she was dirty and sweaty. Mary looked . . . not dirty and sweaty.

Mary said, "I want to see Pete's children." She looked and left. Grace had no idea if Mary was floored by their incredible beauty and intelligence or was grateful that she had dodged a bullet. That reminds me, Loretta Lynn and Conway Twitty recorded a song called "You're the Reason Our Kids Are Ugly." (Hmmm. It can't be my fault. I am incredibly handsome. Moving right along.)

I saw Mary a couple of times from a distance in the next two years we were in Fort Collins. I was usually on my Schwinn riding to work, a college class, or home; and she was driving in a car full of kids, probably hurrying off to dance class, swimming lessons, soccer practice, etc. She'd honk, and I'd wave just like you might do if you saw a friend or neighbor from down the street, or someone from your church. We never actually visited or had the time to get together and were operating in different circles. We were like two ships that had crossed paths in a harbor or the middle of the ocean and then sailed on happily content in the course each had chosen.

Interestingly enough, I never ran into anyone else I had known at Fort Lewis during those two years in Fort Collins.

Life In Fort Collins

One of my class's projects was we made a map of the United States to scale and painted it on the school playground. It was about the size of a basketball court. By the end of the year, my students knew the United States as well or better than eighty percent of the adults in the country.

In the summer we would go for lunch to a little pond alongside the highway. We'd have a picnic and the kids and I would play in the water and Grace would study.

In the winter on many weekends I would drive to Steamboat Springs by way of Laramie. It was a 160-mile drive each way over snowy, icy roads taking about three and a half hours, but the skiing was wonderful. It is still my favorite place to ski. I would sleep in the van on a mattress in a sleeping bag.

One day I got to ski with Hank Williams Jr. Well, he was on the chair in front of me, and I yelled "Hi Hank."

I bet you didn't know he was hard of hearing. That is the only reason I can think of that he would ignore me. I know and have met lots of unfamous people who are also hard of hearing. Sometimes when I yell "HI" they won't hear me and sometimes they will remember something they have forgotten elsewhere and run in the opposite direction.

When things would get too noisy for Grace, she would take her books and go to the Village Inn, order a coffee, and study all afternoon, or long into the night. They got to know her and kept bringing her refills.

She completed her last three years of college in two while still being the best wife and mother a man and two little children ever had.

It was a proud moment for the two of us the day we walked across the stage, and I got my Masters in Guidance and Counseling and Grace got her Bachelors of Science. We loved Fort Collins and gladly would have stayed, but CSU had such a good reputation that there were hardly any job openings and none in her major which had brought us clear from California.

Best of Times/ Worst of Times

I am going to construct my own abbreviation for words in this title: BOT & WOT. The next two years were both. I'll call them "The Best of Times and the Worst of Times: BOT, WOT, and BOTAWOT. If you are reading the book out loud, pronounce them as bought, what, and bought a what. The "A" stands for "and."

While we were in Yucca Valley and Fort Collins, Big Donna, my favorite mother-in-law was asked to become the teacher in the pre-school for the Chichiltah Chapter. With the help of three outstanding people, Larry, Lulu, and Annie. Their school became the top one in the Eastern Agency. (BOT)

Big Donna was asked to take the position of the second person in charge of the whole Eastern Agency pre-school during our last year in Yucca Valley. To do this she had to be in Crownpoint every day, a distance of 100 miles. She tried to visit every school under her at least every two weeks and one of them (Canoncito) was 130 miles away (260 round trip). To make a long story short she was putting on about 80,000 miles a year on her vehicle, a Ford Bronco. She was often far from any kind of help in scary weather and needed a vehicle she could depend on.

Grace and I managed to get on with a small school district in the Colorado mountains. The trouble was we had to find a place that needed both our specialties. We came close in the little mountain community. Although we weren't teaching down the hall from each other like had been our dream job, we were in the same building. Her class was directly over mine on the floor above. I was teaching 5th, my favorite grade and she had junior and senior high school students.

On a visit, Sarge and Big Donna became worried about how far we had to drive in the mountains to get to school. So Instead of turning in her used Bronco, Big Donna gave it to us.

They did not like to think of their only daughter and grandchildren in a snowy mountain town without a 4-wheel drive. Then after that for a few years, she would give us a year old Bronco with 80,000 miles on the odometer , and we'd give her a 2-year-old Bronco with 90,000 on it to turn in.

Abandoned Ski Resort

Less than an hour's drive from the school was a wonderful little ski area. It was near the top of Guanella Pass which runs from 285 to I-70 where it comes out near Georgetown. I read where it got over 300 inches of snow a year.

The first year I was there, I got to drive the school ski bus on weekends. Grace went up as a second in command. She took lessons but never got out of the snowplow stage except for one memorable day near the end of the season.

She and another skier were riding up on the T-bar. (A T-bar is a method of pulling skiers up the hill with their funnies (fannies) resting on the horizontal parts of the upside-down "T". The weight distribution is equally balanced between the two skiers, and the "T's" leg (long part) is connected to the cable above their heads which pulls them up the hill.

They were nearing the top when the person riding with Grace bailed off unexpectantly. This ruined the perfect balance, and Grace who had been unprepared for this started to fall forward. Her outside hand flew out and joined the inside hand on the long part of the T-Bar.

So far, so good. No, so far not so good, so far so terrible. As her teeny tiny little funny slipped off the T, the end caught under her jacket . . . and other upper-body clothing. She was soon being dragged on her stomach up the hill. She let go of the T-Bar, but her clothes didn't. Her arms, still in the jacket, were trapped and she was being pulled through the snow. It was dark inside the jacket and she had no idea what lay ahead. Would she be dragged through the rocks at the top of the lift? She did not know about the safety bar which stops the lift if a skier hits it.

All she could do was scream. And scream she did. I am sure some thought it had something to do with Early Warning System and wondered if we were under attack from Russia. I would not be surprised if she started several avalanches, and if any bears were in the area hibernating, their nap was over.

Up to this point our recollections are pretty much the same. But Grace and I remember the rest of the story differently.

FORGETFUL GRACE WHEATLEY REMEMBERS: The worker on the top of the lift first heard her screams, then saw her being dragged up the hill by what looked to be a ski jacket attached to the T-Bar. He threw on the brakes and rushed over with another worker to see if he could help. It took a few minutes for them to get her untangled, covered, and on her feet. Once this was accomplished, she shoved off as fast as she could from this embarrassing situation. For the first and only time in her life, she skied like the wind for the bottom, fearlessly using a series of stem Christies and and parallel turns.

HONEST GRANT WHEATLEY REMEMBERS: That's pretty good, Grace, but that's not the way I remember the incident.

I had just got on the T-Bar and was near the bottom of the hill when I heard the scream and recognized it immediately. *Oh God*, I thought, *I hope we're not having another baby.* (This was the woman who shut down Yucca Valley and surrounding towns during the birth of our first child.) I recognized that sound, but unfortunately, it was coming from way above me.

My riding companion asked, "DID YOU HEAR THAT?"

Many times in my nightmares., I thought. "No, I didn't hear anything."

He looked at me in disbelief.

"I'm deaf," I said.

"Oh, I'm sorry,' he said. "It sounds like a flock of peacocks being attacked by a pack of coyotes!"

I realized my Boo Boo immediately and beat him to the punch. "I read lips. That's how we're able to have this conversation."

"Oh." (He wasn't too bright but certainly was empathetic.)

After being dragged for a short distance, Grace slipped out of the jacket and rolled out of the way of those on the T-Bars coming up the hill behind her. She managed to get to her feet and stood there shivering. Gone was her jacket, sweater, and ski poles.

Everyone seemed to have a comment as they passed by, and unfortunately many of them were students of hers or mine. Some comments I remember hearing about were:

"Aren't you cold, Mrs. Wheatley?"

"Does Mr. Wheatley know you are doing this?"

"Hubba Hubba."

"Mrs. Wheatley, I think it is against the law to take off your clothes on the ski hill."

"GOOD LORD CRIED THE WOODCHUCK, WHAT IN THE HELL DO YOU THINK YOU ARE DOING?" (That was me.)

"@#$%&*" That was her answer. (I think she learned some of those words from the sarge when they were carrying furniture up the steps at Aggie Village.)

There she stood trying to modestly cover up with her hands and a knitted ski cap. She was only half successful. She needed two ski caps or one big sombrero. Having two children in two years had maximized certain areas of her anatomy. (I offered her my ski cap. I didn't have a sombrero.)

She said, "Give me your jacket or die." I remember thinking, *she is going to make a great Auntie some day, all she needs is a parrot.*

Even though it was cold and windy I made the sacrifice and handed her the jacket. She didn't even say "Thank You." Someone had arrived with her poles. She thanked **them**, then shoved off for the bottom. I could not keep up with her. (I could have, but I fell trying to.)

To the best of my recollection, that was her last time on skis. We made a bargain that night. She didn't ever have to ski again, and I did not have to go to any craft fairs or Hobby Lobbys.

I was asked later to speak with my wife about her conduct and language on the ski hill. I was told that neither were appropriate in front of children, or even truck drivers or motorcycle gangs. One of the Board members even asked me if Grace had been in the Merchant Marines. He hadn't heard some of those words since he was a member of the black gang on a tramp steamer. "Black gang" was the name for those who shoveled coal into the furnaces on the steamships. The dust from the coal would get into their pours and darken their skin.

Geneva Basin is no more. It closed because of financial problems. After several years of being closed, it fell into disrepair. Then when a chair came loose from the cable, the government burned the lodge to the ground. I am not completely convinced that Mrs. Huba-Huba didn't have something to do with the incident.

I read an article where Geneva Basin is now known as Colorado's most famous abandoned ski resort. I am so glad that it was in its hay day when we taught in the community.

Lucky

Back in the days when Tom was four and Donna was two we would fly someplace to meet Sarge and Donna. In those days you would have to walk out to the plane on the tarmac and climb up steps that had been moved out to the plane, like The President still uses today.

The airlines would usually allow (1) the elderly, (2) those with physical problems and (3) those with small children to go first.

On the long walk out to the plane one day, we overtook an old man who qualified in two of the three categories. He was taking baby steps, breathing hard, and bent at the waist. Tommy stepped up and took the man's hand and said "Hello." (I think Tommy thought he could help this man.)

The old man smiled, stood a little taller and asked Tom what his name was. "My name is Tommy and I think you are very lucky."

Suddenly the old man's pace picked up. He stood a little taller. A smile crossed his face as he and the little boy walked together. "How am I lucky, Tommy?"

Tommy said, "You are going to get to see God real soon."

The old man must have been an atheist because he seemed to wilt on the spot. The steps became shorter, the bend greater, and the smile a frown.

Officer Wheatley

Growing up, I had always dreamed of being an engineer on one of the Southern Pacific's orange-sided Daylights. Trains were pulled by large, steam-powered locomotives. People traveled long distances on trains and dressed up to travel. By the time I was ready to join the job market, airplanes had mostly taken over this role.

My son Tom had wanted to be a policeman. By the age of five, he could perfectly imitate the sound of the siren on a police car, only louder. (After all, he was the son of "you know who.")

One day, the kindergarten teacher confronted us on this issue.

"Your son has a siren that is driving me crazy."

"I'm sorry," Grace said. "We'll have a talk with him."

The teacher looked at me expecting more apologies or a stronger remedy. She was disappointed with my answer.

"Have you noticed a measurable drop in criminal activities in your class since Sheriff Wheatley was inserted into the student population?" I asked.

I could tell by the expression on her face that it was already too late. The siren had completed its mission of driving her . . . somewhere.

Square Dance

"Wheatley, you need to become part of the community."

That was my principal talking. He continued, "I see where the Square Dance Group is starting classes next week, and the 4-H needs volunteers. Neither one of these interested me. But I said, "4-H." I pictured myself riding a prancing horse, a golden palomino like Trigger, and brushing him and feeding him some oats or an apple.

Then my mind drifted back to a show and tell of a week earlier. Tim had mentioned how much fun they had castrating pigs last year in 4-H. I thought I knew what castration meant and it wasn't being part of an acting troop.

Was this some kind of sick sport or game played by ranchers? I grew up in the city and that kind of thing, when needed, was done by a veterinarian or Hell's Angels.

"I changed my mind," I said. "I have always wanted to learn how to square dance, even more than I have wanted to castrate pigs."

The principal suggested I go to a dance that weekend and watch and see if I wanted to take lessons. He said the Club, the Ridge Runners, dance on Saturday nights twice a month. After he left I started grumbling. "grumble grumble grumble" I grumbled all day long for three days. On Saturday, the day of the dance, I stepped up my grumbling. BIG GRUMBLE, BIG GRUMBLE, BIG GRUMBLE. I grumbled all the way to the dance.

It was dark when we arrived at the hall. As we walked through the dark parking lot, I could hear the music. It was lively and peppy with a good beat. I could hear laughter and joyful shouts. The music was affecting my attitude. Against my will, I was getting happier.

We got to the door and walked in. The contrast from the outside to the inside was totally amazing: from dark to brilliant. The women were dressed in colorful outfits and looking totally feminine. The men all looked neat with vests that matched their partner's skirts. Some of the men had more badges than a French general.

The man on the stage, the caller, was calling out commands to the beat of the music and the dancers were moving in unison to those commands with smiles on their faces and shouts of YAHOO when they were returned to the one dressed in the same colors as them (their partner). Miraculously everyone ended up with their partner in the spot they had started from and at the same time. I later learned this was called "patter."

I figured that was the end of that dance and wondered why the folks were still staying on the dance floor as if waiting for something instead of rushing to the table full of refreshments and snacks or a bench to rest.

I spotted the parents of some of the kids in my class out on the floor. I had really enjoyed visiting with them at PTA, I went out on the floor to say "Howdy."

(The caller had been looking through his stack of records. He found the one he wanted, put it on the turn table and dropped the needle). This would be what they called a singing call. I learned the hard way that each session (called a tip) consisted of a patter and a singing call. I was trapped in the middle of the hall dodging whirling, twirling, shouting humans. Not knowing the names of the calls, I had no idea of which way to dodge until the last second as I tried to negotiate my way across this minefield of dancers to the sidelines and my wife.

The record the caller had chosen was "Mary Ann Regrets," a favorite song of mine. I had worn out two records of it with Burl Ives singing, but I couldn't believe my ears. I liked this version much better. It was faster and had a strong beat. I noticed that my feet were tapping along in time with the music. Dave Smith, the caller, had a great voice. **I was sold on square dancing.** It was love at first hear. All the male pigs were safe from me.

They announced that lessons would start on Wednesday. I tried to sign up and pay, but they wouldn't let me. They said they didn't take the money until after the third lesson because everyone wasn't able to do it and it only took one person not doing it right in a square to cause the square to break down.

The next week we drove into Denver and went to a wonderful mall called Cinderella City and then to a square dance shop. I bought several books on learning to square dance. Nothing was going to stop me from being a square dancer. Grace bought us two matching outfits. We chose the brightest, most-colorful outfit in the store. I later learned that outfit had been in the store for three years without even a nibble.

When the lessons started there were about three squares of students (24 people). Only two of them wore square dance outfits. Even the club members that had come to help (called angels) wore normal clothes. When the caller saw us, he said he would have to go out to the car and get his dark glasses. He started calling us Rhinestone and Diamond Lil.

The next Week we wore the dullest clothes we could find. Our new goal was to have people look at us and yawn. It worked for Diamond Lil. She became Grace, but I couldn't shake the Rhinestone moniker, as in, "Rhinestone where did you get those bright red socks?" (Oops. I thought *the dude must have x-ray vision. My Levis should have hidden them.*)

All night it was, "Rhinestone, do you know which side is your left and which side is your right? Okay Rhinestone, let me give you a hint. It's the side you put your watch on."

The hint helped. Whenever I heard "right" I'd think of my watch. When the caller would call a "left" anything, this was easy for me. I would think of the hand I write with because I am a southpaw. I got through that night on "pens" and "watches."

We were told in advance, that on the night of graduation, to pass the class and join the club we could only accumulate 10 errors, and the club officers would be evaluating and grading us. (I don't remember anyone not making it. I think they just said that to scare us and make us study and work harder.)

Badgers

Another thing I noticed was a lot of them had earned badges. To name a few there were badges for square dancing on the grass, dancing in a jail, dancing in an intersection, dancing seven days in a row, dancing without touching, etc., etc. I love a challenge. I decided Rhinestone was going to have more badges than anyone else in the club.

At our graduation, Caller Dave said the best thing we could do was get dancing experience and dance to different callers. At that time, a person could dance somewhere every night of the week in Denver, and Denver was less than an hour's drive. Dave also called for two other clubs.

A square of us decided to impress him by showing up at those clubs. We were also a little nervous about dancing with strangers. We caravanned down to the city in two cars. There were eight of us. We lost our nerve and decided to square up together every tip.

On the way home after one of the dances, Lou said, "Do you realize we have earned the badge for dancing four nights in a row.

"Wow!" said I. I was stoked, especially after Lou's wife said, "There is a badge for dancing seven days in a row."

I was excited. Too excited to think. "How many more days do we need to get that one?"

"Duh," said Grace,

"Duh," said Lou.

"Duh," said Lou's wife.

"What?," said I.

"Three," said Grace.

"Three," said Lou's wife.

"Oh," said I. (Did I ever mention that math was not my best subject?)

The four of us decided that one week was within our reach, and we reached it. Lou's wife, a noted trouble maker, said there is a badge for dancing two weeks in a row, and we may never get this close again."

"She has a point," I said. "No one in the club has one of those badges."

Lou's wife said, "I don't think they make one for more than that."

"Thank God," said Grace.

Lou said, "If we keep going, we only have seven more days to go. But if we stop we will be 14 away."

I thought to myself, *I wouldn't want to do a whole week again, let alone two weeks*. It had been a strain with the hour in and the hour out after teaching school all day and preparing lesson plans. We reluctantly agreed to go for the second week. Those in the other car said we were lunatics and they wanted no part of every night for two weeks. They were perfectly happy with the seven day badge. It is just a coincidence that their car earlier had scored higher on an intelligence test I found in *The Reader's Digest* than ours.

They say confession is good for the soul. I don't believe it, but I will check-out my soul at the end of this next paragraph.

We might have done a little fudging on our way to the record. Rule One said you had to dance to a live caller. It did not say how many tips you had to dance. We left several dances early and on a couple of occasions we went to a caller's house after midnight, woke him up and had him call us a tip. A tip after midnight gave us a span of 48 hours (essentially two days) to get the next tip in.

I was not able to find my uh soulometer, but I have just taken my temperature, blood pressure and pulse. Last night I slept like a baby and didn't wake up once. I am willing to state with almost 100% confidence, that confession has neither helped nor hurt my soul. Please forget what I wrote in the previous paragraph. Ignore the confession.

A new factor was added. The people that made the badges became good friends and enthusiastic encouragers. They even went to many of the dances with us and joined us waking up callers. They even promised to invent a badge for whatever day our streak ended. It showed a calendar with all the days crossed off and said gone but not forgotten. At the end of thirty, we all took a three-week break.

By the end of the 2nd week, the four of us had more badges than anyone else in the club and were plotting on ways to get the other two to drop out so we could be sole possessors of the record. It had become an unspoken contest of endurance, which ended in a tie at thirty. Grace and I had to settle for being the best looking couple in the Denver area with the brightest outfits. Too bad there wasn't a badge for that.

Dilemma

We got word that Sarge was having health issues and started applying for teaching positions closer to them. They had been so good to us and helpful, we decided that now it was our turn to be the adults. We obtained positions at the boarding school in Crownpoint, NM with help from Big Donna. Crownpoint is only ninety miles from the ranch.

It was at Crownpoint we achieved our dream. We were teaching junior high and her classroom was right next to mine. We would come out into the hall and visit between classes. She was teaching science and I was teaching language arts. **BUT**

There was a fly in the ointment . . . a big fly . . . a dragonfly . . .I named him Pegasus. In fact, there were several flies. I will number them for you.

Grace did not enjoy teaching and did not want to do it for the rest of her life.

Sarge's health was getting worse. The doctors determined that he needed to move to a lower altitude. The ranch is at 6,800 feet above sea level. That is fifteen hundred feet higher than Denver. He was planning on moving to Phoenix where the elevation was around 1,000 feet.

Uncle Bob was wanting to retire and neither one of his daughters wanted the business. One owned a bookstore in Gallup and the other was a surgical nurse in Albuquerque.

Migration

A bean farmer from the area who I will call Swenson started spending his winters in Apache Junction. There was not much to do there in those days when the Greyhounds weren't running, but go to the furniture auction on Saturday night and the flea market during the day.

Swenson came back with a tan, extra money, and telling glorious tales about a land where there was no snow in the winter and nearly everyone was from his and Bob's generation.

Uncle Bob went down, fell in love with the country, and bought a piece of land with a small cinder block house on it. This was three blocks from where Swenson had land. They told the Sarge and Big Donna that there was a vacant lot across the street from their property and it was for sale at a very reasonable price. He and Betty planned on spending weekends down there and letting other family members use it when they weren't.

The sarge bought the lot across the street planning on putting a mobile home on it. He had always wanted to live in Phoenix and called it God's Country.

We bought the land two doors down and had it fenced in so we could take our dogs with us and not keep them tied up on visits. At the time we owned two Airedales.

We had two good years working in Crownpoint at the boarding school. The pay was good, the rent was cheap, and if you needed to keep a child after school you just sent a note to the dorms.

Weekends were spent out at the ranch 90% of the time. We would leave the school on Friday after classes. Saturday mornings we would help Bob and Betty in the store.

The store was open 5 days a week plus half a day on Saturday. Saturday afternoons were spent puttering around doing necessary changes and repairs. Saturday, evenings after supper we would go over to Bob and Betty's and listen to tales of how it had been growing up out there. Bob was a wonderful story teller. There was no television in Cousin's valley because the signal went right over the top of the cliffs. Both houses had shelves loaded with books.

We had been talking about taking over the store **someday,** but put it off because I liked what I was doing, and we were making great money working for the B.I.A. Then one day after we'd been there two years, Bob said, "It's **Someday.**"

It was "Sh-t or get off the pot day." The store made more than either one of us, but less than the two of us. I wanted to stay on the pot at least another year . . . or two, but Bob said he would either sell it or close it. He wanted to retire while he was still healthy enough to enjoy retirement.

I voted to stay teachers and apply to places like Alaska, Hawaii, Steamboat Springs, Las Vegas, Durango, and Yucca Valley. Grace voted for the Trading Post and Cousins Valley. The thing that tipped the balance was the kids.

As teachers, we had seen how those living in towns and cities had lost control of their kids who would get in trouble after school hanging out at the malls, or in gangs, and were more influenced by peer pressure and television than parents. I, myself, got into a few misadventures growing up. Living out at the ranch, the kids would ride the bus home from school and contain any mischief to our 160 acres. Because of the red cliffs causing the signal to go over our heads, they would not be influenced by television. In the ranch house, they would be living in a land of books.

I gave in. I did not completely capitulate by voting for the store, I abstained (did not vote). That way I was able to save face and maintain my position as head of the family. The store won by a vote of 1 to 0. It was a close election (a squeaker).

Unfortunately, a family member had to be 18 to vote and show proper identification like a passport or driver's license. That left the kids out. Why do I say, unfortunately? Because I learned later if the little ones were allowed to vote, I might be writing this in Maui as a retired school teacher.

The real adventures in our lives begin in the next book. Pete, Grace, and a couple of tadpoles become Indian Traders in the checkerboard area of the Navajo reservation. You are definitely invited to join us. I hope you do.

For the moment, the working title is "Cousins Brothers Nephew and Niece." Why? Well, Grandpa Charlie Cousins started the first trading post, and he had four boys, all of which at one time or the other helped in the store. One of the brothers (Bob) took over after Charlie retired. Then Bob's niece (Grace) took over when he retired. How did I worm my name in? Simple. It is my typewriter.

Sincerely,

Your Pal Pete

Wild Bill

Map

Tom, Huck and Aunt Polly

CSU Graduation

Diamond Lil

ABOUT THE AUTHOR

Peter Grant Wheatley was born in Miss Frelse's Maternity Home: 1939 in Bakersfield, California. He was not anxious to leave the womb, earning him the nickname "Peter the Procrastinator" and making an enemy of his mother and the doctor during the eighteen-hour struggle. After the doctor had had his shot at Pete's fanny, she declared it was her turn. She had to be restrained by several nurses and two large orderlies.

His writing career started in elementary school where he earned the attention of adults with an award winning essay: "The Reson Peter Wazn't in scul.Yeasterday."

In Yucca Valley as an adult Pete edited the popular "Desert Wind." His work has been featured in the international "American Square Dance Magazine." For over 30 years his column was the most popular in the state magazine: "The Southwest Dancer."

Mr. Wheatley's working career started at the age of six in 1945 selling the Sunday Los Angeles Times from his wagon. In high school, he worked after school as a cleanup person in a bakery, and during the summer as a caddy at the golf course, and a fast-food cook. He has also been a bus driver, over-the-road truck driver, driller's assistant, rough neck, geophone placement engineer, cook and crew on an LST, dormitory proctor, U. S. Marine Reserve, school teacher, Indian trader, and now published author. Other than his inability to hold a job he is known for his sense of humor.

Mr. Wheatley has been in love with and married to the same women for 57 years. With her help, he is working on his third book.

Things happen to Mr. Wheatley and he has the ability to write about them in a humorous manner. His wife thinks he's funny, so does his cousin Susie (sometimes). So you should buy his book. They both can't be wrong.

www.ingramcontent.com/pod-product-compliance
Lightning Source LLC
Chambersburg PA
CBHW060019100426
42740CB00010B/1537